SHRUBS

MICHAEL DIETSCH

SHRUBS

AN OLD-FASHIONED DRINK FOR MODERN TIMES

The Countryman Press
A division of W. W. Norton & Company
Independent Publishers Since 1923

DEDICATION

To Jennifer, Julian, and Mirabelle

Shrub is a colonial-day drink whose name is derived from the Arabic word sharab, to drink. It is a concentrated syrup made from fruit, vinegar, and sugar that is traditionally mixed with water to create a refreshing drink that is simultaneously tart and sweet. In the nineteenth-century, the drink was often spiked with brandy or rum.

—Entry in The Ark of Taste,
Slow Food Foundation

CONTENTS

FOREWORD

Amateur historians with a thirst increasingly populate the drinks world—bartenders, brewers, writers, and chefs keen on digging through the past with a pen in one hand and a glass or a jug in the other. This is much as it should be—for while the food world has largely had an unbroken history, with everything from *Larousse Gastronomique* to generations of Italian grandmothers passing food knowledge over the ages, the drinks world (especially once you stray far from wine) has had few such institutions.

Of course, beer, cocktails, and other libations have faced challenges that the food world hasn't. While food and drink are both regularly buffeted by wider outside forces as well as the ever-changing whims of taste, the drinks world has also encountered blowback on political and religious fronts, with everyone from the Woman's Christian Temperance Union to Andrew Volstead and Prohibition's politicians messing with the stuff that flows into our cups. But while many of today's history-oriented spelunkers are bartenders digging up the bibulous knowledge buried by Prohibition, they're also finding a common interest with these early temperance advocates: the flavorful (and non-alcoholic) class of drinks called shrubs.

The shrub family tree can be traced back to Roman times, and this pre-refrigeration manner of preserving seasonal produce had a particular resonance throughout the Colonial era and into the earliest years of the new republic—and decades later, they were briefly revived by temperance advocates looking for liquor-free alternatives that offered a more flavorful oomph than, say, lemonade. Repeal and world war washed shrubs away again, but more than a half-century later, after the food science–mad mid-twentieth century, Americans began to rediscover taste—and along with it, the manner through which our ancestors approached their food and drink.

Shrubs are now every bit a part of our contemporary culinary landscape as much as the spread of artisan cheesemakers and the boom in high-tech kitchen gadgetry. But shrubs hold a distinctive place in our glasses, occupying a hybrid position between Colonial-era rusticity and innovation-driven change. And, in a move surely to the chagrin of Prohibitionists, shrubs have found particularly fertile terrain in today's craft-cocktail bars, where their acidic bite and fruity brightness are used to doctor bespoke cocktails, as well as spark the non-alcoholic side of the menu with a little excitement.

It's hard to toss a cocktail shaker nowadays without hitting a bartender featuring at least one house shrub on their cocktail menu—and even some of the more settled and staid restaurants around the country are livening up their non-alcoholic drink menus with kitchen-made shrubs that promise exponentially more flavor and character than do ho-hum commercial sodas. And since the initial release of this book in 2014, many of those vinegar-pouring shrubmakers have used Michael Dietsch's *Shrubs* as a source—at first for recipes and information, but eventually as inspiration for venturing in their own fruit-rich directions.

Few would have likely figured that these mixtures would find such enthusiastic reception, but Dietsch and his shrub-filled soaking jars have tapped a particular moment in the storied zeitgeist. If you're new to the shrub scene, there's no better source for getting started than the book you hold in your hands—and if you've been down the shrub path before and are looking for fresh ideas, Dietsch has you covered there, as well. But before you take a sip from that first glass, be sure to raise a toast and give a word of thanks to Michael Dietsch for putting today's shrub wheels in motion.

Paul Clarke

Author of *The Cocktail Chronicles*, executive editor of *Imbibe* magazine

INTRODUCTION

The word *shrub* calls to mind a short, stemmy, woody plant, similar to a bush but maybe even a bit bushier. It also refers to a delicious vinegar-based syrup that makes any drink—alcoholic or not—more refreshing. That's the shrub I'm talking about.

I remember the first time I had a shrub. I was in New Orleans for Tales of the Cocktail, in July 2008. Tales of the Cocktail is a cocktail festival held in the French Quarter. It attracts bartenders, distillers, brand representatives, writers, and the general public for five days of seminars, dinners, competitions, tastings, and product launches.

Bartenders around the country were just beginning to rediscover the shrub, and that day I tasted a cocktail by a Chicago bartender named Bridget Albert. Albert is the author of *Market-Fresh Mixology*, and she holds the position of director of mixology for Southern Wine & Spirits of Illinois. Her drink featured cachaça, a Brazilian liquor made from sugarcane juice that's somewhat similar to rum. She also used raspberry shrub, lime juice, and ginger ale. The drink was balanced and refreshing, with no single ingredient taking over. I could taste the cachaça, the fruit, and the tang of the vinegar, but they were harmonious. And since I had just walked into the hotel from a blistering New Orleans summer day, the drink was also the most refreshing thing I had tasted all day. I kept going back for more.

It turns out that vinegar is incredibly good at quenching your thirst when it's hot out. Research shows that sour-tasting beverages—such as vinegar and lemonade—are better at stimulating salivation than are other drinks. A wet

I went on a shrub-making frenzy. I made shrubs out of every type of berry I could find, plus peaches, apricots, nectarines, and cherries. I had so many shrubs in the fridge at any given time that it was hard to fit anything else in there.

mouth helps you feel hydrated even after you're done drinking.

Salivation not only makes you feel hydrated, it stimulates the appetite. Salivation usually indicates to your stomach that food is forthcoming, and therefore it primes your digestive juices to get ready to work. Shrubs are a perfect cocktail to prepare you for a night of fine dining.

When I got home, I had to re-create the drink because I knew my wife would love it. Unfortunately, raspberry season had ended in my area, and I couldn't reproduce the raspberry shrub. However, I was able to find blueberries and gooseberries, so I cooked up my version using those ingredients.

I was right—my wife loved it, and we both fell in love with shrubs.

From that point on, I made them frequently. We drank them in cocktails, we drank them with vermouth or sherry, and we drank them without alcohol, just topped with soda or seltzer. During the summer of 2010, I went on a shrub-making frenzy. I made shrubs out of every type of berry I could find, plus peaches, apricots, nectarines, and cherries. I had so many shrubs in the fridge at any given time that it was hard to fit anything else in there.

My wife would open the door and a bottle of shrub would nearly tumble out onto the floor. She'd shoot dirty looks and sardonic comments my way. But I had the last laugh. In 2011, we found out we were expecting our first child, and those shrubs helped sustain her through her pregnancy when she couldn't drink alcohol.

One of the joys of shrubs is that they're both an adult beverage and a soft drink at the same time. The blend of fruit and tartness is challenging for a lot of children to appreciate, so shrubs tend to appeal more to adults than to kids (although if your kids enjoy shrubs, you've got the coolest kids in the neighborhood). But just because shrubs are "adult" doesn't mean you need to serve them in a boozy way for them to be tasty. The balance of sweet and tart is sophisticated and complex enough that they're wonderful with just soda.

We in the United States have a rich food heritage, and a history of creatively cultivating plants and animals for food purposes. But that culture is shrinking, and many of the foods our grandparents and their grandparents ate are disappearing, either through biological extinction or cultural neglect. Since 1996, the organization Slow Food has been working to develop an Ark of Taste, a catalogue of heritage foods that are in danger of extinction. The shrub is catalogued in this collection.

The Ark of Taste aims to save these foods and call attention to their plight. A food might appear on the Ark of Taste because it's an endangered species, as are certain plants and animals, or it may simply be at risk of being forgotten. Shrub falls into the latter category. The ingredients are plentiful, so there's no risk that shrub is in danger biologically. In fact, the rise of shrubs in popular culture has never been felt more keenly than it is today.

Eric Felten provided the spark in July 2006, writing about Independence Day barbecue beverages for the *Wall Street Journal*. He noted that one of the very few places you could find shrub on a menu was City Tavern in Philadelphia, where it's served with rum, brandy, or champagne. He discussed the thirst-quenching potential for shrubby drinks at Fourth of July cookouts, and provided a recipe. But then he concluded, "why bother when Pennsylvania's Tait Farm makes luscious Shrub syrups in a variety of flavors, using their own fresh fruit vinegars?" (More on Tait Farm to come.)

Felten's cocktail column was always intelligent, well informed, and witty. As the craft-cocktail movement gathered steam in the first decade of this millennium, his column was pored over by cocktail enthusiasts, writers, and

bartenders. So when the idea of shrubs arose in his column, people who study cocktails jumped on it. In 2007 and 2008, shrubs started to gain some steam as ingredients for cocktails, appearing in blog posts, in beverage and bar-industry magazines, and on cocktail menus.

Toby Cecchini then picked the topic up for the *New York Times* in 2008. Cecchini is a bartender and writer in New York City, and he helped developed the drink that we now know as the Cosmopolitan (see my shrubby take on the Cosmo on page 237). He wrote a piece for the *Times* Style section about the surprising deliciousness of vinegar-based cocktails.

It's impossible to overestimate the speed with which the Internet

Vinegar drinks are more than just a cocktail trend, however. They're also common in Southeast Asian cuisine. Andy Ricker is the chef and owner of Pok Pok, a Thai-influenced restaurant with locations in Portland, Oregon, and New York City. Ricker put drinking vinegars on his menu when he opened his eatery. The vinegars were so popular that he now sells bottled versions of them, called Som. The Som line of drinking vinegars includes apple, ginger, honey, pineapple, pomegranate, raspberry, tamarind, and Thai basil flavors. Pok Pok's cocktail menu includes a variety of drinks that feature the Som vinegars.

spreads new or revived ideas in the cocktail/bartending community. When a new product or ingredient hits the market, it seems that within a week, people are already posting cocktail ideas using that product.

A San Francisco bartender named Neyah White started serving shrubs in low-alcohol cocktails, with dry sherry or vermouth. This turned out to be a smart idea. The fruitiness of shrubs pairs very well with dry wine-based aperitifs.

I've provided nearly fifty recipes here for shrubs, and if you follow them to the letter, I know you'll have good results. But I urge you to experiment. Shrub making isn't like baking, where you need to follow the recipe precisely to ensure perfect bread or cake. Shrub making is more intuitive. You can fly by the seat of your pants while making shrubs and still have something delicious to sip. Want more vinegar? Add it gradually until you're happy. More fruit? Go for it. Think

You can fly by the seat of your pants while making shrubs and still have something delicious to sip.

it should be sweeter? It's your shrub, so that's your decision. I believe you can't really go wrong with these recipes. Add an herb if you want. Toss in a pepper if you think it's appropriate. (A hot pepper is probably more suitable with, say, a tomato shrub than it is with kiwifruit, but your tastes might vary.) You can even make your own vinegar, using wine (or cider, or even beer) and starter culture, but I've never made my own vinegar, so I have no advice to offer on that topic.

THE HISTORY OF SHRUBS

Shrubs might be trendy right now, but the idea of drinking vinegar is ancient. Vinegar, of course, is made from wine (and later in the book, I'll describe how it's made). Wine has been around for at least 8,000 years, and because wine naturally turns to vinegar as it ages, vinegar then must be nearly as old as wine. Archaeologists have found vinegar residues in urns and pots from ancient Egypt from about 4,000 years ago, and historians have written records of its use in China dating back at least 3,000 years.

Vinegar served a couple of important roles as a beverage in ancient times. First, people drank it simply so they wouldn't have to throw it away; when you work very hard for your food and beverage, you don't waste it. More importantly, however, vinegar was used to sterilize dirty water, to make it drinkable.

Take, for example, posca. Originally a medicinal tonic used in Greece, posca was a drink made of sour wine or vinegar, mixed with water and flavoring herbs. Roman soldiers and members of lower social classes drank it as an everyday beverage. (Members of higher social classes, of course, drank wine.)

Water of the time was often undrinkable, spoiled by dangerous bacteria. Spiking water with soured wine was a way to sterilize the water while reusing wine that would otherwise be wasted. Posca also provided calories and hydration, and thanks to the vitamin C in the vinegar, it was an antiscorbutic, meaning it prevented scurvy.

Vinegar appears throughout the Bible. The Old Testament's Book of Numbers speaks of the Nazirites, men and women set apart from the general population and consecrated to God. The Nazirites were forbidden to drink wine, other alcoholic beverages, and vinegar. In the New Testament, all four gospels tell the story of Roman soldiers twice offering sour wine or vinegar to Jesus during his crucifixion. The first offering was a blend of vinegar and gall, a narcotic herb that would have eased his suffering. He declined. Later, the soldiers offered him a drink from their own rations of vinegar. This was very likely posca, and he accepted.

How does the Arabic *sharāb* lead to shrub? A lexicographer named Eric Partridge supplied the answer in his 1958 book *Origins: A Short Etymological Dictionary of Modern English*. Partridge traces the history thusly: *Sirab* (or, as Partridge spells it, *sharāb*) derives from the Arabic *shariba*, to drink (verb). *Shariba* also gives rise to *sharba*, a drink (noun), which then gives rise to *sharbat*, the Persian fruit-juice drink, and finally to *sorbet* and *sherbet*. *Sharāb* also enters Middle Latin as *sirupus* and *syrupus*, giving rise to our modern word *syrup*.

Finally, *sharāb* yields another form that means a drink (noun), *shurb* which eventually became *shrub*.

The shrub you drink derives from the Arabic word *sharāb*, or beverage. Using shrub to denote a beverage may seem surprising to you, but you're probably familiar with a few other words that ultimately derive from sharāb—sherbet, sorbet, and syrup.

Shrub, as a word for a beverage, can itself mean two things: The type of shrub I'll be primarily discussing is a beverage made of acidulated fruit juice (fruit plus vinegar), sugar, water, and other ingredients. However, a blended drink made of fruit juice, sugar, and a spirit such as rum or brandy served cold and diluted with water is also known as a shrub.

Shrubs came from Turkey and Persia, in the form of sherbets. These days, we usually take *sherbet* to mean a frozen dessert. Originally, though, sherbets were beverages enjoyed by teetotaling Muslims, made of sugar combined with citrus juice, violets or other flowers, herbs, or nuts. Sherbet has been called the world's first soft drink, arising in a pre-refrigeration era when the only way to preserve fruit juices was to douse them heavily with sugar, alcohol, or vinegar. Because Islam teaches forbearance from alcohol, sugar-based sherbets became popular throughout the Middle East.

Trading ships and travelers brought sherbet back to Western Europe starting in the middle of the seventeenth century. The word went through various permutations, and alternative spellings came and went. The spelling that survived was *shrub*, which came to denote a syrup of citrus and sugar, blended with either rum or brandy, and served aboard trading ships and naval vessels. This form of shrub reached colonial America, where it was popular with such notables as Martha Washington, Benjamin Franklin, and Thomas Jefferson.

At the same time, another very old beverage was gaining steam in the colonies: a fruited, non-alcoholic vinegar beverage enjoyed as a thirst quencher on hot days. This beverage was known first as fruit vinegar. For example, recipes made of raspberries, vinegar, and sugar were called Raspberry Vinegar. By the mid-1800s, however, the word *shrub* was appropriated to describe them, and raspberry-vinegar syrups became known as both Raspberry Vinegar and Raspberry Shrub. Today, of course, we think of raspberry vinegar as a condiment made by taking raspberries, making wine from them, and then turning that wine into a true vinegar; in the eighteenth and nineteenth centuries, though, a raspberry vinegar was simply a vinegar flavored with raspberries.

Vinegar-based shrubs evolved alongside the alcohol-laced versions; some early American cookbooks, for example, offer recipes for both Raspberry Shrub and Raspberry Vinegar. The former drink would be a rum- or brandy-based concoction, and the Raspberry Vinegar would be the vinegary drink we know today as shrub.

The earliest reference to a drinking shrub that I've found is from an itinerant pastor and scholar, Franciscus Junius (1591–1677), a student of old Biblical texts and the evolution of the Germanic family of languages.

At the time of his death, Junius had left many works unpublished, among them his magisterial *Etymologicum Anglicanum*, one of the earliest etymological dictionaries of the English language. As the title implies, the book was written in Latin, which was common for scholarly works of the time.

Junius's work influenced many later lexicographers, including Samuel Johnson, whose *A Dictionary of the English Language* became the primary source for

English etymology when it was published in 1755. (Incidentally, Johnson himself described the beverage form of shrub as "A spirit, acid, and sugar mixed.")

The date of the *Etymologicum*'s writing is uncertain, but Junius died in 1677. His *Etymologicum Anglicanum* was finally edited and published sixty-six years after his death, in 1743, by another lexicographer, Edward Lye. Lye took the liberty of inserting editorial comments into Junius's work, as such:

> SHRUB, *a liquor, "most pleasant," says Junius, "The name arises from the East, whether from Syrian sareb; or from Arabian sirab."*
>
> *"Junius rightly notes that sharab means to drink; and shorb, the thing itself that is drunk; hence our shrub, an intoxicating drink of dry wine, golden fruit, and sugar mixed together."—a very pleasant liquor, made generally with rum or brandy.*

As I mentioned in the introduction, shrub, as we know it today, arises from a Turkish beverage, sherbet. The philosopher Francis Bacon provides one of the earliest known references in English to sherbet, in 1627:

> *They have in Turkey and the East certain confections, which they call servets, which are like to candied conserves, and are made of sugar and lemons, or sugar and citrons, or sugar and violets, and some other flowers; and some mixture of amber [ambergris] for the more delicate persons: and those they dissolve in water, and thereof make their drink, because they are forbidden wine by their law.*

What Bacon encountered wasn't a drink, but instead a tablet of sugar, flavored with fruit juice, flowers, and ambergris (a form of whale cholesterol; yes, it's rather gross, and no, I don't have any recipes that call for it). These sherbet tablets were made by Turkish confectioners, who would take boiled sugar syrup, add flavorings such as fruit juices or essential oils, and then pour the syrup into molds or onto marble slabs, where it would cool and solidify.

When you wanted to drink a sherbet, you'd take a sherbet tablet and let it dissolve into water. In *Sherbet and Spice: The Complete Story of Turkish Sweets and Desserts*, Mary Isin tells of a German confectioner who visited Istanbul in the 1830s and found sherbet tablets flavored with "orange, cinnamon, rose, lemon,

vanilla, salep (orchid root), pistachio, bitter almond, violet, jasmine, opium, barberry, strawberry, sour cherry, pomegranate, sour grape, apricot, peach, plum, date, pineapple and chocolate."

Sherbet entered Europe in the sixteenth century, by way of Venice, which for much of its history was a prosperous trade center between Western Europe and the Islamic world. Traders and merchants brought all manner of goods to Western Europe, including sherbet. From Venice it spread to the rest of Italy, France, and all of Europe. By the nineteenth century, sherbet was quite trendy in England. In 1813, Lord Byron wrote of it, "Give me a sun, I care not how hot, and sherbet, I care not how cool, and my Heaven is as easily made as your Persian's."

In 1655, an Anglo-Welsh historian named James Howell published a book recounting his travels. In one passage, he discusses the beverages of various countries—the ales and beers of England and Germany, the "usquebagh" (whiskey) of Scotland, and the mead of various European countries. Speaking of the "Turk," which here appears to be a general term for Muslims, and not a name suggesting residents of Turkey, he writes of their abstinence from wine and spirits, and then speaks of the beverages they drink instead, including a "Sherbet made of juice of Lemon, Sugar . . . and other ingredients."

Sometime during the sixteenth or seventeenth centuries—no one's quite sure of the date—a drink called switchel arose in the Caribbean. In its original form, it was made of vinegar, ginger, molasses, and water. Landowners discovered that their slaves were drinking rum while working, and switchel became a cheaper substitute. The molasses trade carried it to colonial New England by the late 1600s, and eventually honey came to replace the molasses. Switchel was served to farmers, especially at hay-harvesting time, which is why it's also known as haymaker's punch. The vinegar helped to cool the farmers during the heavy labor of harvesting hay, while also quenching their thirst.

In his 1787 *Letters on Egypt*, Claude-Étienne Savary writes of being served sherbet at a meal. Savary was a student of Middle Eastern culture and was fluent in Arabic. He wrote a life of Muhammad and a French translation of the Quran. "Sherbet," he says, "comes from the Arabic word *shorba*, which signifies beverage. It is composed of lemon juice, sugar, and water, in which perfumed paste is dissolved, made from the excellent fruits of Damascus; they usually mingle a little rose-water. It is a most agreeable beverage, the nectar of the orientals, and drank only by the great, or people in office. I was several times presented with it on my visits to the governor of Damietta, and drank it with pleasure."

Sherbet even made its way as an entry in the third edition (1797) of the *Encyclopaedia Brittanica:*

> SHERBET, or Sherbit, a compound drink, first brought into England
> from Turkey and Persia, consisting of water, lemon juice, and sugar, in
> which are dissolved perfumed cakes made of excellent Damascus fruit,
> containing an infusion of some drops of rose water. Another kind of it
> is made of violets, honey, juice of raisins, &c.

So what do sherbet and shrub have in common? And what distinguishes each from the other?

I think the answer, at least in eighteenth-century England, was pretty simple. Sherbet was a beverage made of lemon juice, water, and sugar. In some cases, perfumed cakes were added and allowed to dissolve, and in some cases, rose water was added.

Shrub was lemon or orange juice, water, sugar, and—here's the salient difference—rum or brandy. The cocktail historian David Wondrich, in his 2010 book *Punch*, says, "The term of art for the mixture of sugar and citrus juice upon which [p]unch is constructed is variously given as as 'sherbet' or 'shrub.'. . . 'Shrub' is also used to refer to the same thing, but with some or all of the spirits added." As Wondrich alludes, the word shrub was slowly taking on the meaning of a sweetened fruit juice with added alcohol—sort of a spiked lemonade.

This raises the question, how did alcohol come to enter shrub in the first place? I can't find a definitive answer to this. An amusing story describes smugglers in Southwest England bringing barrels of rum to the Cornish coast, encountering customs agents, and sinking the barrels to avoid discovery. This rum, so the story goes, took on so much seawater that the hooch was unpleasant to drink, and so innkeepers and saloon owners would mask the taste with sherbet.

> The story about using shrub to mask the taste of seawater-tainted rum might be simply an amusing fiction, but I do think there's an element of truth in it.

I can't find any verification for this story, or any primary sources to back it up. A company called Phillips of Bristol sells a bottled shrub cordial, and the Cornish-smuggler story is part of its marketing, so I take it with a large grain of Cornish sea salt. The story does, though, have some anecdotal evidence in its favor. First, Cornwall remains one of the few places where rum-based shrubs have never waned in popularity. Not only do Cornish taverns continue to offer the beverage, but a Cornish singing group, called the Rum and Shrub Shantymen, tours the countryside performing old sea shanties, sea songs, and traditional folk music.

The story does have one other thing going for it—seawater or no seawater, rum in the 1600s and 1700s was a rough-tasting product. This shouldn't be surprising; it was still in its infancy. Although no one knows exactly when rum first appeared, historians think it arose no later than the early seventeenth century. In his book, *And a Bottle of Rum*, Wayne Curtis discusses several possible origins: Barbados in the early 1600s; Hispaniola or Cuba, at about the same time; Brazil; or even fifteenth-century Europe. Whatever evidence existed about rum's birth, that evidence is gone.

What we do know is that by the mid-1600s, rum was all over the New World. We have records from Dutch, English, Spanish, and French sailors and colonists regarding their encounters with rum. Rum's marriage with shrub, then, happened while both were still very young.

Why was this early rum so foul? Wayne Curtis has the answer. Whereas brandy is the distilled essence of wine, and whiskey is that of beer, rum is "the distilled essence of industrial waste," he writes. Rum is distilled from molasses, which is left behind during the process of making sugar. Early distillation methods were crude and imprecise, and so the quality of rums varied from batch to batch, and from distiller to distiller.

The story about using shrub to mask the taste of seawater-tainted rum might be simply an amusing fiction, but I do think there's an element of truth in it. I find it entirely reasonable to assume that drinkers first used shrub to mask the flavor of harsh rum, whether that rum was ever dumped into the sea or not.

Shrub reached colonial America by no later than 1716, when an expedition by the Knights of the Golden Horseshoe set out from Colonial Virginia to

By 1737, shrub was common enough to be shipped into New York Harbor.

explore the west. The sixty-three-person group must have been thirsty; they carried "Virginia red wine and white, Irish usquebaugh [whiskey], brandy, shrub, two sorts of rum, champagne, canary, cherry, punch, water, cider, etc."

What was this early shrub? From the 1736 edition of the *Dictionarium Britannicum*, we have an early definition: "[A] compound of brandy, the juice of Sevil oranges and lemons kept in a vessel for the ready making of punch at any time, by the addition of water and sugar."

The *Dictionarium* was the work of Nathan Bailey, among the earliest English lexicographers, even earlier than Edward Lye. Bailey first published an English dictionary in 1721, his *Universal Etymological English Dictionary*. The third edition of that work, from 1726, contains only references to botanical shrubs: bushes, small trees, and whatnot. The *Universal Dictionary* was, as implied by the name, a holistic English dictionary, covering words from across the language. His *Dictionarium*, by contrast, was a book of technical terms and less common words.

In 1737, the *Historical Register* takes note of a duty laid in New York on the importation, by ship, of rum, brandy, or other distilled liquor or shrub. So by 1737, shrub was common enough to be shipped into New York Harbor.

A 1752 book, published by the colony of New York, lists the laws of that colony dating back to 1691. Among the laws in the book are various duties and tariffs placed on items imported into the colony. Shrub is mentioned in several of the duties, but this is the first reference:

> *An Act to let farm the Excise of Strong Liquors, retailed in this Colony, for the Time therein mentioned, and for declaring Shrub liable to the same Duties as distilled Liquors. Pass'd the 20th of September, 1728.*

Now, how do you make the stuff? In 1737, we see one of the earliest known recipes for shrub, from the second edition of *The Complete Family-Piece*, by an anonymous author. It calls for two quarts of brandy, the juice of five lemons (and the peels of two), nutmeg, white wine, and sugar. (I've included a modernization of the recipe on page 80.) A 1772 French work, *Dictionnaire Universel*, provides the following definition for *sharāb: Mot Arabe qui signifie le vin et meme toutes les liqueurs fortes.* In English, "Arabic word for wine and even all strong liquors."

The *Oxford English Dictionary* picks the tale up from there. It defines shrub as a "prepared drink made with the juice of orange or lemon (or other acid fruit), sugar, and rum (or other spirit)." Its first citation is from a 1743 work, *English Housewifry*, by Elizabeth Moxon, which gives instruction on making Orange

Scurvy was first identified as early as 1500 BCE. As Europeans began exploring the world by ship, stories arose of entire crews falling to scurvy. The disease even plagued the voyages of Vasco de Gama and Ferdinand Magellan, each of whom lost hundreds of men. Because the powers of Europe were looking at exploration to provide economic and political expansion, not just captains and ship owners but also governments and physicians were desperate to contain scurvy.

By 1593, the English admiral Richard Hawkins was recommending the use of citrus to prevent scurvy, but no one yet understood why, nor was citrus widely adopted after his recommendation. Through the seventeenth and early eighteenth centuries, the use of citrus to prevent scurvy began to pick up, but it wasn't until 1747 that citrus's scurvy-fighting properties were finally proven. The Scottish physician James Lind conducted what's now seen as one of the first clinical trials, judging citrus's efficacy versus that of sulfuric acid, vinegar, seawater, cider, and barley water. He published his results in the 1753 book *A Treatise on Scurvy*. The British Navy slowly started to adopt the practice of providing citrus, and by 1795 had virtually eliminated scurvy.

Shrub. Her recipe calls for the juice and peels of Seville oranges and lemons, sugar, and brandy. (A modernization appears on page 83.)

The OED's next citation of shrub comes from *Gentleman's Magazine*, October 1747, in a long piece about methods for preserving the health of seamen on long naval voyages. We know now that scurvy is caused by the lack of vitamin C in the diet. Vitamin C is crucial to the diet because it helps us to make collagen. Without collagen, tissues begin to break down, leading to such symptoms as muscle and joint pain, lethargy, anemia, swelling in the body, ulceration of the gums, and even the loss of teeth. Left untreated, scurvy can be fatal. Unlike most animals, humans are unable to synthesize vitamin C, and so we need to consume it in our diets in order to stay healthy.

> A mixture of lemon juice and rum (shrub as they call it) may be carried in any quantity

To promote the health of sailors, an anonymous correspondent to a 1747 issue of *Gentleman's Magazine* suggests equipping ships with ample supplies of cider; vinegar; and fresh apples, lemons, and oranges. Should the long-term storage of fruit prove impractical, the writer suggests, "a mixture of lemon juice and rum (shrub as they call it) may be carried in any quantity, as it will keep a long time."

Straying from the OED, we find other early references to shrub. From 1751, we find an entry from the department The More Things Change. *The Student, Or, The Oxford and Cambridge Monthly Miscellany* published a note on a friend of the publication's, one Ashley, who apparently established a punch house of which the young Oxbridgers were quite fond. They write:

> *Nothing can be more agreeable, than to give encouragement to extraordinary merit. We are therefore very glad, that the notice taken in our last of the celebrated Ashley, and his* Punch-House, *has in any wise attracted the attention of the public. We acknowledge to have received*

(*accompanied with a cag [keg, presumably] of excellent shrub) a very polite letter from that eminent retailer of warm rum.*

Elizabeth Cleland, writing in her 1755 book, *A New and Easy Method of Cookery*, provides the following recipe for shrub:

> *To Make Shrub.*
>
> Take *five English Gallons of Rum, three Chopins of Orange and Lemon-juice, and four Pounds of double-refined Sugar; mix all together, but first pare the Rind of some of the Lemons and Oranges, and let them infuse in the Rum for six Hours: Let all run through a Jelly-bag, then cask it till it is fine, and bottle it.*

A chopin, if you were wondering, is not a Polish composer of music, but a Scottish unit of liquid measurement, equivalent to eight gills. Oh, that probably doesn't clear things up either. A gill was five fluid ounces, and so one chopin equaled probably about forty ounces. The measure of a gallon, as if eighteenth-century units of measurement weren't confusing enough, varied depending on whether you were in England, Scotland, the colonies, or, I suppose, the canals of Mars. An English gallon would have been about 160 fluid ounces. (A US gallon, by contrast, holds 128 ounces.)

Another shrub recipe comes from 1760, from a book titled *The House-keeper's Pocket-book, and Compleat Family Cook*, by Sarah Harrison. Hers calls for brandy, lemon juice and peels, and sugar.

As noted earlier, the use of shrubs on seagoing vessels arises in the middle of the eighteenth century, as a 1761 reference from *Dodsley's Annual Register* shows. An essay titled "Useful Hints for Sailors and Seafaring Men" concerns itself with providing tips to keep old salts healthy on long oceanic passages. Among its advice is to prescribe a little shrub after a day of hard labor, to guard "against putrefaction."

A 1762 advertisement in the *London Chronicle* offers several delicious choices available at the James Ashley Public House and Cellars, on Ludgate Hill, in London: Jamaica rum, cognac, Batavia arrack, and orange shrub.

A 1763 reference comes from *Dodsley's Annual Register*, from a harrowing account of a ship's voyage. The *Phoenix*, captained by a fellow named McGacher, left London for Africa, where it picked up 332 slaves, and then headed to the

"Potowmack" in Maryland. On Wednesday, October 20, 1762, the *Phoenix* encountered a storm, and the ship sustained heavy damage. Every cask in the hold was smashed to pieces, save a barrel of flour; 10 pounds of bread; 25 gallons of wine, beer, and shrub; and 25 gallons of spirits.

In keeping with the nautical theme, shrub appears in Patrick O'Brian's series of historical naval novels, featuring the nautical adventures of Captain Jack Aubrey and his ship's physician, Stephen Maturin, during the Napoleonic Wars of the early 1800s. *The Ionian Mission* (1981), for example, features a recipe for a hot lemon shrub, similar to hot toddy.

The recipe itself is simple; it appears in *Lobscouse & Spotted Dog*, a gastro-nomic companion to the O'Brian novels. It's much on the same order as the recipes of the early 1800s: lemon zest, lemon juice, sugar, and rum are combined and left to age for about a week. When it's time for service, you pour some into a mug and top with boiling water.

In 1764, Daniel Bellamy's *A New, Complete, and Universal English Dictionary* defines shrub as "spirit, acid, and sugar mixed."

More recipes for shrubs follow, including a 1769 recipe for almond shrub. This recipe differs from previous ones in that it calls for a pint of milk, which is mixed with brandy, orange juice, lemon peels, loaf sugar, and bitter almonds. The milk is allowed to curdle, and then the solids are strained off until the shrub runs clear. A currant shrub follows, using similar techniques. This business of allowing the milk to curdle may sound revolting, but it's common practice in making milk punches, and this almond shrub sounds a bit like an early version of the latter.

From 1777, two recipes for shrub come from *The Lady's Assistant for Regulating and Supplying Her Table*, by Charlotte Mason. The first is an orange shrub typical of the time, consisting of Seville orange juice and peels, rum, and sugar. The next is one of the earliest recipes for currant shrub, using currant juice, sugar, and either rum or brandy.

A 1791 recipe for double rum shrub comes to us from a Scottish writer, known only as Mrs. Frazer, who compiled a cookbook called *The Practice of Cookery, Pastry, Pickling, Preserving, Etc.* Mrs. Frazer calls for sugar, lemon and orange juices and peels, and rum. What makes it "double rum" is that you use some of the rum to steep the peels in and add the rest to the sugar and citrus juice.

Early recipes for such things as gooseberry vinegar and raspberry vinegar are virtually identical to today's recipes for vinegar-based shrub

SHRUB IN THE NINETEENTH CENTURY

The dawn of a new century, 1800, brings a double shot of shrub from a book called *The Complete Confectioner*, by a Mrs. H. Glass. Mrs. Glass brings us first a citrus shrub, named for Sir John Cope, an eighteenth-century British general. This shrub calls for brandy, lemon juice and peels, white wine, and sugar. As for Sir John, there's no evidence that he had much interest in shrubs, but history has given us a chance to play punnily with words. Among Cope's descendants are two recent American presidents, both named Bush. And this is the only joke I'll make in this book about shrubs and bushes.

Mrs. Glass, however, also has a recipe for currant shrub, calling for ripe white currants, rum or brandy, and sugar.

The first references to what we would now consider a vinegar-based shrub come to us not as shrub recipes, but as "quick" fruit vinegar recipes, just at the turn of the nineteenth century. I say "quick" because a true fruit vinegar is a time-consuming process: you press the fruit to make juice, ferment the juice to make wine, and then ferment the wine to make vinegar.

The "quick" fruit vinegar recipes you see in early cookbooks generally involve steeping fruit in vinegar for a time, and then straining it off. Early recipes for such things as gooseberry vinegar and raspberry vinegar are virtually identical to today's recipes for vinegar-based shrub—that is, they consist of fruit of some kind, vinegar, and sugar.

Take, for example, this recipe from 1804's *The New Practice of Cookery, Pastry, Baking, and Preserving*, published in Scotland by a Mrs. Hudson and a Mrs.

Donat, which I'm quoting in full just so you can see how similar it is to a modern raspberry shrub:

> *Raspberry Vinegar*
>
> *Fill your jar with raspberries, and cover them with vinegar; let it stand 24 hours, and drain it off and strain it; to every pint add one pound of sugar, put it in a jar, and set that in a pot on the fire till the vinegar has boiled some hours; take care to keep it close covered that no water from the pot gets in; the best way is to have hay about it; it must be covered with a bladder while in the warm bath; when cold, bottle it and cork it very close; when it begins to look tawny, it is done.*

The New London Family Cook (1808), by Duncan MacDonald, offers a similar recipe, along with advice toward its use:

> *Raspberry Vinegar Water.*
>
> *Put a pound of fruit into a bowl, pour on it a quart of the best white wine vinegar, the next day strain the liquor on a pound of fresh raspberries, and the following one do the same, but do not squeeze the fruit; drain the liquor as dry as you can from it. The last time pass it through a canvas wetted with vinegar. Put it into a stone jar, with a pound of sugar to every pint of juice, broken into large lumps; stir it when melted, then put the jar into a saucepan of water, or on a hot hearth, simmer and skim it. When cold bottle it.*
>
> *This is one of the most useful preparations that can be in a house, not only as it affords a refreshing beverage, but being of singular efficacy in complaints of the chest. A large spoonful or two in a tumbler of water. No glazed or metal vessel must be used for it.*

An 1808 book, *A New System of Domestic Cookery*, offers a very similar recipe. Raspberry vinegars were often touted in old books for their medicinal uses, especially to slake the thirst of those fighting fevers or colds. In 1817, a physician named William Kitchiner published a cookbook called *Apicius Redivivus; Or, The Cook's Oracle*, in which the good doctor offers two recipes for raspberry vinegar:

Raspberry Vinegar. (No. 389.)

Put your raspberries into a stone jar, tie them down, and set them in a slack oven for four hours; press out the juice, and add to each quart three pounds of fine loaf sugar, boil and skim till it comes to a syrup. Boil a drachm of bruised cochineal in a pint of white wine vinegar for fifteen minutes; when cold, add to it the quart of syrup, a quart of cold vinegar, and a quarter of a pint of rectified spirit of wine.

Raspberry Vinegar, another way. (No. 390.)

Take fine fresh gathered red raspberries well picked; put them into a wooden or china bowl, with as much good distilled wine vinegar as will cover them; bruise and stir them frequently for four days; strain them, and to every pint of the liquor add a pound of lump sugar: boil for a quarter of an hour, taking off the scum as it rises; add to each pint a glass of brandy, and bottle it: when used, it may be mixed in about eight parts of water, and is a most excellent cooling beverage to assuage thirst in fevers and colds, &c., and is agreeable to most palates.

Samuel Frederick Gray was a British botanist and pharmacologist. In 1818, he published *A Supplement to the Pharmacopoeia*, providing instruction to pharmacists about how to produce compound medicines. Gray's recipe, from the 1828 fourth edition, for raspberry vinegar is telegraphic (like all the other formulas in his book), but easy enough to understand: "Raspberries 3 lb, vinegar 2 pints, white sugar 3 lb: produce 3 pints of vinegar."

An 1819 issue of the *Monthly Gazette of Health* published the remarks of a "Lady Bountiful" (a pen-name, one presumes), writing from Essex with advice for parents of children suffering from measles. The correspondent speaks of the importance of keeping the child warm, inside and out, by providing hot-water bottles and warm tea or, if the child prefers, raspberry vinegar in warm water.

Margaret King Moore, writing in her 1823 *Advice to Young Mothers*, also emphasized the therapeutic aspects of raspberry vinegar: "The moment a child complains of a sore throat, a piece of flannel should be put around the neck, the feet bathed at bed-time, and some warm acidulated liquor given before the child

goes to sleep. Lemonade, currant jelly or syrup of raspberry vinegar and water, or honey and water with a very few drops of good vinegar, would be suitable for this purpose."

As useful as shrubs and "quick" vinegars were for fighting scurvy, measles, and sore throat, though, they seem to have excited another ailment in some of its partakers. *The London Literary Gazette and Journal of Belles Lettres, Arts, Sciences, Etc.* published an excerpt of the 1827 memoirs of an Irish judge, Sir Jonah Barrington. The good jurist recalls the drinking behaviors of some of his colleagues:

Even now, shrubs can be useful for those who are sick. Recall what I said earlier in the book: Sour-tasting beverages, such as vinegar and lemonade, are better at stimulating salivation than are other drinks. When I interviewed Kim Tait, of Tait Farm Foods, for this book, she recounted a story in which an oncology nurse praised Tait Farm's shrubs for helping chemotherapy patients stay hydrated while experiencing the dry mouth that chemo brings on.

> *I have heard it often said that, at the time I speak of, every estated gentleman in the Queen's County was honoured by the gout. I have since considered that its extraordinary prevalence was not difficult to be accounted for, by the disproportionate quantity of acid contained in their seductive beverage, called rum shrub—which was then universally drunk in quantities nearly incredible, generally from supper-time till morning, by all country gentlemen, as they said, to keep down their claret.*

Even *The Lancet* gets in on the healthy-vinegar action. In an 1828 review of the book *The Good Nurse*, the renowned medical journal excerpts a section of the book in which the anonymous author discusses ways to help a feverish patient fall asleep. One suggestion is to administer a cooling liquid, such "raspberry-vinegar and water, or lemonade."

From William Augustus Henderson's 1829 book, *Modern Domestic Cookery and Useful Receipt Book, Adapted for Families in the Middling and Genteel Ranks of Life*, comes a recipe that also plays up the purported medicinal aspects of

Cookbook writer Lydia Maria Child was the first person to use the word shrub to describe a drink made of fruit juice, sugar, vinegar, and water. She was a novelist, essayist, abolitionist, poet, and feminist. In her writings, she opposed white supremacy, slavery, male dominance, and American expansionism, while championing Native American rights. You might not know her name, but there's a good chance you know at least some of her poetry. If you recall the Thanksgiving song that begins, "Over the river and through the wood, to Grandfather's house we go," you're familiar with her most famous poem.

raspberry vinegar, stating that it's "grateful to the palate" and effectual for "complaints in the chest."

The first person to use the word *shrub* in the way we use it today was a cookbook writer named Lydia Maria Child. She used it to describe a drink made of fruit juice, sugar, vinegar, and water. Thanks to her appropriation of the term, and thanks too to the rise of Prohibition in America, through the remainder of the 1800s, we see fewer and fewer boozy shrubs in cookbooks and recipe collections, and more of the vinegar-based versions.

Among Child's writings was the *Frugal Housewife*, published in 1829. (In later editions, she renamed it *American Frugal Housewife* because there already was a *Frugal Housewife* book in Britain.) Cookbooks and household-advice books of the time were generally meant for upper-class households with servants. Child, though, aimed to teach an economy of housekeeping, a way of tending to the home without wasting anything. She encouraged thrift and self-reliance.

Economy seems to be at the heart of her shrub recipe, in that she offers shrub as a substitute for fortified wine:

> *Raspberry shrub mixed with water is a pure, delicious drink for summer; and in a country where raspberries are abundant, it is good economy to make it answer instead of Port and Catalonia wine. Put raspberries in a pan, and scarcely cover them with strong vinegar. Add a pint of sugar to a pint of juice; (of this you can judge by first trying your pan to see how much it holds;) scald it, skim it, and bottle it when cold.*

Child was no temperance advocate; *American Frugal Housewife* contains references to brandy, rum, wine, and other alcohol, for drinking, cooking, and cleaning. It seems reasonable to assume, then, that she used vinegar in her shrub as a gesture of frugality, and not one of temperance.

Through the first few decades of the nineteenth century, boozy shrub recipes abound, and all of a similar, familiar technique: take some fruit juice, add sugar and rum or brandy, store it for a few weeks, and then bottle it up for service.

But after 1840, vinegar-based shrubs proliferated. *The American Housewife* of 1841 (by an anonymous author) provides an example of both types of recipe. First, there's a currant shrub, which calls for strained currant juice, sugar, and brandy. A recipe for lemon shrub also calls for brandy. But a recipe for raspberry shrub offers a twist:

> *Raspberry Shrub*
>
> *To three quarts of fresh, ripe raspberries, put one of good vinegar. Let it remain a day—then strain it, and put to each pint a pound of white sugar. Boil the whole together for half an hour, skim it clear. When cool add a wine glass of French brandy to each pint of the shrub. A couple of table-spoonsful of this, mixed with a tumbler two-thirds full of water, is a wholesome and refreshing drink in fevers.*

By the 1850s, rum shrub had made its way not only to the United States but also beyond, and even all the way to Hawaii. A Honolulu newspaper, the *Pacific Commercial-Advertiser*, published advertisements in 1856 and 1857 from a shipping firm, D.C. Waterman, offering brandy, Jamaican rum, gin, Champagne, Sauterne, Boker's bitters, and rum shrub. A similar ad appeared in the newspaper *The Polynesian*, offering brandy, gin, rum, sherry, port, wines of various types, and rum shrub.

Vinegar has long been a folk remedy for various ailments, including coughs, colds, and fevers. It was also used to clean and sanitize wounds.

I talked earlier about the role that posca played in hydrating centurions, but it wasn't just Roman soldiers who were issued vinegar rations; the Union Army in the American Civil War received them as well. Diaries and letters of soldiers are full of accounts of their rations. One infantryman wrote to a friend in 1861 that, "Our rations are not of the most palatable kind, but rather of the substantial and consists of the following articles: pork, fresh beef, rice, coffee, beans, hard and soft bread, and vinegar. We receive beef, rice, and soft bread every alternate day."

Recipes for raspberry vinegar—as well as punches and cocktails using it—appear in the 1864 *How to Mix Drinks* (also known as *The Bar-Tender's Guide*, and *The Bon-Vivant's Companion*) by pioneering barman Jerry Thomas, and in the 1862 *Manual for the Manufacture of Cordials, Liquors, Fancy Syrups, &c. &c.*, by Christian Schultz.

An 1871 book, *The Reminiscences of Fifty Years*, by a Scotsman named Mark Boyd, speaks of his life as a businessman and his role in promoting the colonization of Australia and New Zealand. In the book, he writes of attending funerals in his native Scotland, where guests enjoyed port, various baked sweets, sherry, brandy, a round of whiskey, and then to close, either rum or shrub. Hmm. I've never been to such a funeral.

An 1873 recipe from the *Presbyterian Cook Book*, a charity cookbook from the First Presbyterian Church of Dayton, Ohio, might be expected to be a temperance drink. In that same year, the Woman's Christian Temperance Union was founded in Hillsboro, Ohio, so prohibitionist intent was clearly in the Buckeye State's air at the time. The book contains two recipes for shrub, one for currant and one for raspberry. The currant shrub calls for brandy, whereas the raspberry calls for cider vinegar.

Just a few years later, though, the Buckeyes were a little less bibulous. *Buckeye Cookery*, by Estelle Woods Wilcox, compiles recipes from the ladies of Marysville, Ohio. Its recipe for raspberry shrub calls for cider vinegar.

As late as the 1880s, a drinker could still find rum shrub on offer in fine Manhattan hotel bars, however, as an anecdote in an 1888 issue of the *New York Evening World* shows. The *Evening World* published a column called Caught in the Eddies, and subtitled Passing Phases of Men and Things in the Great Metropolis. The idea was to play up weird and unusual occurrences in New York.

In this case, the story concerned an Irish terrier who could apparently walk on his hind legs, while smoking a pipe. The dog's owner invited several passersby to join him in a hotel barroom, where the dog performed several other tricks. "He was given 10 cents," the paper says of the dog, "which he held in his mouth, and was asked if he would take a rum shrub, cocktail, gin fizz, sherry cobbler, brandy smash or whiskey straight. At the words 'Whiskey straight' up jumped the dog, gave a succession of sharp yelps and running behind the bar dropped the dime into the barkeeper's hand. He refused to touch the whiskey, however."

Oh, for the days of straight whiskey for a dime.

As late as 1900, recipes for raspberry vinegar appeared in such

In the "Who Knew?" page of your diary, add "Bloomingdale's had a wine department." In an advertisement that ran in April 1895 issues of the *Evening World* and the *New-York Tribune*, the venerable department store promoted several items for sale through its wine department, including rye and bourbon whiskey, ale and stout, brandy, vermouth, and rum shrub (this sold for $5.00 a gallon).

publications as the *New York Times*, which published this formula in its Women Here and There—Their Frills and Fancies column:

> *A good raspberry vinegar is made by allowing one pint of vinegar to three quarts of raspberries. Let the berries stand in the vinegar for three days, when they should be mashed and the mixture strained. To each pint of the juice, add one pound of sugar, and boil twenty minutes. Bottle when cold. Allow a spoonful to a glass of water.*

The food writer Amanda Hesser adapted that recipe in 2010, for her Recipe Redux column in the *Times*, and again that same year for her book, *The Essential New York Times Cookbook*.

Vinegary shrubs appealed greatly to temperance-era drinkers, those who were abstaining from alcohol but still wanted something to drink.

Vinegary shrubs appealed greatly to temperance–era drinkers, those who were abstaining from alcohol but still wanted something to drink. *Good Housekeeping* magazine wrote in 1903 that "Gooseberry shrub makes a delicious 'winey' temperance drink," and gave a recipe that called for cider vinegar, ripe gooseberries, and sugar.

By the time of this 1903 recipe, of course, the temperance movement was in full swing in the United States. Several states had passed their own laws prohibiting the sale and consumption of alcohol, and the nation as a whole was only seventeen years from enacting the Eighteenth Amendment, providing for national prohibition.

During this period, the medicinal uses of shrubs continued to find some play in print. *Practical Druggist and Pharmaceutical Review of Reviews*, from 1909 and 1910, offers two alcohol-free recipes for shrub. If the source, a periodical for pharmacists, seems odd, keep in mind that at the time, many druggists still operated soda fountains. The first is for a pineapple shrub, and it calls for pineapple syrup, grape juice, and lime juice. The second is a generic fruit shrub, calling for raspberry and pineapple syrups, vanilla, grape syrup, and citric acid.

By 1909, some writers were aware that they were using two names— raspberry vinegar and raspberry shrub—for the same beverage. Writing in *The Spatula*, a magazine for druggists, an E. F. White provides a recipe for Raspberry Shrub Syrup to be used at a drugstore's soda fountain. White writes, "This is also called Raspberry Vinegar Syrup."

You see more evidence of this awareness in an August 1920 recipe, from a Mrs. T. B., of New Brunswick, New Jersey. She wrote to the Tribune Institute newspaper column, a regular piece in the *New York Tribune* that taught homemaking principles, asking for a recipe for Raspberry Vinegar. The editor, Virginia Carter Lee, responded by writing, "Raspberry vinegar or raspberry shrub is one of the most refreshing of summer beverages," and offered two recipes.

A 1911 recipe, from *Good Things to Eat*, by Rufus Estes, offers another vinegar shrub. Estes, a former slave, was a Pullman Car porter, as well as a chef for U.S. Steel in Chicago. Estes's book is historically interesting because he offers a brief sketch of his life, in which he discusses working as a slave, attaining his freedom, working to support his mother, and eventually, entering the Pullman service in 1883. Estes has recipes for currant and raspberry shrub, each of which uses vinegar.

Not that *all* recipes of the early twentieth century were temperance recipes: a Saint Louis bartender named Tom Bullock published a recipe for brandy
shrub in his 1917 book, *The Ideal Bartender*. Bullock, incidentally, was the first
well-known African American bartender; he worked at the Pendennis Club in
Louisville before moving to Missouri and taking a job at the St. Louis Country
Club, where he served nationally influential politicians and businessmen. One of
his patrons—George Herbert Walker, forebearer to two American presidents—
wrote the introduction to Bullock's book. In 1920, in the early days of Prohibition, a cook named Bertha Stockbridge wrote a cocktail book aimed at the
teetotaling drinker. She tells her readers, "The hostess of to-day will be called
upon to serve drinks in her home more than formerly, I imagine, and it were
well to go back to the habits and customs of our grandmothers and be prepared
to serve a refreshing drink in an attractive manner at a moment's notice. To do
this, one needs have a stock of syrups, either homemade or commercial, as well
as a supply of shrubs and vinegars on hand."

The hostess of today will be called upon to serve drinks in her home more than formerly, I imagine, and it were well to go back to the habits and customs of our grandmothers and be prepared to serve a refreshing drink in an attractive manner at a moment's notice.

Stockbridge's book overflows with recipes for fruit ades, ices, and punches;
teetotal cocktails, sours, and juleps; shrubs and fruit syrups; ginger, maple, and
root beer; milk drinks (both cold and hot); coffee and cocoa; and desserts such as
sundaes and sorbets. By the early twentieth century, vinegar-based shrubs were

enjoyed nationwide. Newspapers across the country either ran recipes for fruited vinegars or shrubs, or published advertisements for establishments selling them. The Library of Congress offers a trove of historic American newspapers as part of its *Chronicling America* website. Searching the database turns up recipes or advertisements from all parts of the United States: a 1922 recipe for raspberry shrub from Mount Vernon, Ohio, for example; a 1913 recipe from Albuquerque, New Mexico; and a recipe from Saint Paul, Minnesota. In addition, newspapers in Chicago; Philadelphia; Burlington, Vermont; Richmond, Virginia; Oklahoma City; Ogden, Utah; Wenatchee, Washington; and Donaldsville, Louisiana, all mention shrubs or fruited vinegars in one way or another.

SHRUB DISAPPEARS . . . AND RETURNS

By about the end of Prohibition, shrub in both forms—boozy and not—was disappearing from America and Europe. Why? Three things did it in, I believe, but first recall why shrub was ever popular in the first place. It arose from sherbet, a non-alcoholic beverage enjoyed by alcohol-abstaining Muslims. Similarly, the non-boozy version became popular among Prohibitionists in nineteenth-century America. So shrub and sherbet, as early soft drinks, appealed to people who chose for whatever reason not to drink alcohol.

At the same time, shrubs (boozy and not) and sherbets were a great way to preserve fruit. Sugar, alcohol, and vinegar are all preservatives.

Once the world's navies found other ways than punches and shrubs to get vitamin C into a seaman's daily diet, the use of shrubs on naval vessels completely

> Now, when I say that shrub "disappeared," I don't mean to imply that it disappeared entirely from American foodways.

died out, and the boozy shrub then slowly died out among landlubbers in England and America—in the latter country in part due to Prohibition, as I've shown.

The end of Prohibition, the rise of carbonated soft drinks, and the development of refrigerators and freezers then pushed out non-boozy shrubs. Teetotalers could get Coca-Cola and its derivatives at any drugstore soda fountain or in bottles and cans, and their fruit stayed fresher longer when chilled.

Now, when I say that shrub "disappeared," I don't mean to imply that it disappeared entirely from American foodways. Had that been the case, I wonder whether modern bartenders would have ever "rediscovered" it. Shrub stuck around in certain small communities, and one such small community, the Pennsylvania Dutch, seems to have rescued it from obscurity.

As you might know, the name Pennsylvania Dutch is a little confusing, in that they're not Dutch in the way we use the word today—they're not from the Netherlands. Instead, they're the descendants of various groups of German, Alsatian, and Swiss settlers who arrived in Pennsylvania starting in 1683.

Now, shrub isn't a traditional drink of Switzerland or Germany, as far as I can tell, so the Pennsylvania Dutch didn't preserve the tradition out of a sense of continuity with their homelands. No, I think something else happened here. As raspberry vinegar (later called raspberry shrub) became a common beverage in colonial America, the Pennsylvania Dutch happened to be among the colonials who adopted the drink. However, the Pennsylvania Dutch are generally a group who like to preserve their food traditions, and once raspberry vinegar/shrub became part of their tradition, they kept it, alongside lemonade, birch beer, and other foods.

And I suspect it's because of their influence that the drink is now known as raspberry shrub and not raspberry vinegar. Pennsylvania Dutch cookbooks retained the shrub name, and so when the drink was due for its revival, it came back as shrub.

Just as the word shrub came to mean a vinegar-based beverage in the nineteenth century, the word took on yet another culinary connotation, this one apparently arising from Southern cooking. Menus from the 1950s, '60s, and '70s offer something called a shrub, but in this case, it wasn't a beverage.

The Day, a newspaper from New London, Connecticut, described a 1954 luncheon in Washington, D.C., put on to celebrate the opening of the Washington

Antiques Fair. On the menu were a variety of historical Virginian recipes: Regent's punch, southern frosted fruit shrub, Williamsburg fried chicken, asparagus hollandaise, Williamsburg baked tomatoes, and queen of puddings. The reporter, Sigrid Arne, described the shrub as "just a fruit cup chilled with a sherbet."

Menus of the time generally listed these sorts of shrubs either at the top of the menu, along with appetizers, fruit cups, and juices, or as a palate cleanser between courses of a multi-course menu. The Dearborn Inn and Clinton Inn of Greenfield Village, in Dearborn, Michigan, offered a luncheon in 1963 for a food and wine society called the Confrérie de la Chaîne des Rôtisseurs. The luncheon was suitably splendid, at least if the menu is any indication. After a soup course, the luncheon kicked off with whitefish, followed by stuffed quail. Diners took a brief break to enjoy lemon shrub before tucking into the lamb course. Next, in Continental style, came a salad course. Then came peaches and "dainty pastries from the almond brittle basket" and finally java paired with port or sherry.

In the 1970s, Wiggins Tavern in Northampton, Massachusetts, offered a cranberry shrub, described on the menu as cranberry juice with "tavern-made sherbet." And as recently as 1989, the King's Arms Tavern in Williamsburg, Virginia, offered a similar shrub—in this case a fruit cup with apricot, pineapple, and grapefruit juices topped with lemon or orange sherbet. Even now, tasting menus at certain restaurants feature a bit of house-made sherbet, sometimes in fruit juice or sparkling wine, as a mid-course palate cleanser, but it's seldom called a shrub.

SHRUB REEMERGES

Today, we're in the midst of a shrub renaissance, as mentioned in my introduction. Bartenders around the world are using them in cocktails, chefs are using them in sauces and marinades and salad dressings, and home cooks are whipping them up for yummy drinks, both boozy and non. Some of the credit has to go to Tait Farm Foods. Tait Farm has been making shrubs since 1987, and it was Tait's shrubs that the *Wall Street Journal* columnist Eric Felten discovered back in 2004, launching the modern shrub revolution.

Tait Farm is located in Centre Hall, Pennsylvania, in the central part of the state. The Taits have long been known in the area for the specialty food products they make from produce from their own farm and from other local farmers. Back in the late 1980s, farmer David Tait had a bumper crop of raspberries. He froze them to sell in the winter, but he realized he still had far too many to sell. He started to wonder how he could repurpose them into a value-added product. A friend mentioned to him an old recipe for raspberry shrub, from a

Mennonite cook named Betty Groff, who wrote about Pennsylvania Dutch recipes.

The Taits began to sell their shrubs at farmers' markets and health-food stores, mostly just within Pennsylvania and the surrounding area. I talked to David Tait's wife, Kim Tait, who took over the business after his death in 1997. "For years," she told me, "we put a lot of effort in marketing shrubs as a culinary syrup." She developed recipes for sweet and sour cabbage, ginger carrots, sweet pickles, blueberry salsa, and grain and bean salads, all using Tait Farm shrubs.

How does Kim Tait like to enjoy her shrubs? In sangria, especially on a hot summer day. She makes hers with 12 ounces of white wine, 12 ounces of seltzer, and 4 ounces of fruit shrub.

HOW TO MAKE A SHRUB

Quarter to eight in the evening, and you and your date are at a nice restaurant, getting ready to peruse the menu. Your waiter tells you that the bartender has a new cocktail, made from tequila, rhubarb shrub, and lime juice. The drink sounds good, so you try it and you love it. Because you enjoy getting crafty in the kitchen, you decide to try making shrubs at home.

Good decision. Making shrubs at home is fun, and although there are a few folks out there making them professionally, bottled shrubs can still be hard to find in some cities. Moreover, shrub making is a great way to get creative and try various flavor pairings, and it's an excellent way to use seasonal produce as it arrives at your grocery or farmers' market: the first strawberries of early spring; peaches and plums in the summer; tomatoes, tomatillos, apples, and pears in the fall; and oranges in the dead of winter.

Generally speaking, there are two different methods for making shrubs—a hot process and a cold process. I started shrub making using the hot process, but I've largely switched over to the cold process. In the hot process, you put crushed fruit, sugar, and a little water into a pan on the stovetop. You cook the ingredients until they form a syrup. Let the syrup cool and then drain out the solids and discard them. When the syrup is cool, combine it with vinegar and store it in the refrigerator.

The cold process works somewhat differently. You make syrup by combining

"When a shrub ages, it's like an ecosystem. Ambient yeast (that is, the yeast on the fruit itself and yeast from the air) turns the sugar into alcohol, and the Acetobacter (the bacteria in unpasteurized vinegar) turns the alcohol into more vinegar. In this symbiotic relationship, the Acetobacter feeds on the yeast's metabolic waste products, and this removal then stimulates the yeast to continue to make alcohol. Eventually this will stabilize and not turn the whole shrub into fruit vinegar, since the bacteria-induced pH change will stall out the yeast's fermentation process (and thus the bacteria's acetic acid-producing pathway). The end result will be a different flavor profile than just the initial fruit, vinegar, and sugar blended mixture; this change would be comparable to how fresh-pressed grape juice morphs as it becomes wine due to the microbial byproducts such as polyphenols created during the ferment."

—FREDERIC YARM, PhD biochemist whose love of drink history and science led him to become a cocktail writer and professional bartender by trade.

fruit and sugar in a bowl, and leave them alone for a day or two to have some fun together. The sugar draws out the juices of the fruit and forms syrup. You then strain out and discard the solids and, finally, add the vinegar.

Each process has its advantages. The hot process is faster; you can generally complete the shrub within about an hour, whereas the cold process can take up to three days, depending on how long the fruit and sugar need to commingle. (Of course, during most of that time, you're not actively working on the shrub; the amount of time you spend actively making shrub is about the same with either method.)

The cold process, however, has a game-changing advantage, at least in my opinion: it doesn't cook the fruit. By leaving the fruit raw, the cold process allows the full flavors of the fruit to come through, fresh and unmuted. I've tested hot-process shrubs and cold-process shrubs side by side, and I always find that I prefer the vibrant flavors of the cold-processed ones.

There is a third method, which involves putting fruit into a jar, pouring boiling vinegar over the top, and letting that steep for a few days, shaking the jar every day to redistribute everything. I've tried that, and I find that this method also mutes the fresh fruit flavors you get from the cold process.

Finally, there's yet another method, one that involves steeping the fruit in cold vinegar for a certain amount of time, and then boiling the fruit-infused vinegar with sugar. I haven't tried that method, but again, since you're boiling everything, I have to assume this method loses the freshness of the fruit.

As an example of some of the creative ways you can pair flavors in shrubs, look at some of the offerings from Shrub & Co., a Berkeley, California, company that makes shrubs for bars and home mixologists.

Shrub & Co. offers a variety of flavors: Spicy Ginger; Grapefruit; Apple; Peach; Wildflower Honey; Cranberry with Douglas Fir; Blood Orange with Cardamom; and Strawberry with Meyer Lemon.

The Shrub & Co. team is Juan Garcia; Juan's wife, Deborah Marskey; Matt Bruns; and Matt's wife, Marianna. Juan is a classically trained marketer and former consultant to the beverage industry, Deborah is involved in her family's farming business, Matt has a culinary and bartending background, and Marianna is a violinist and yoga instructor with many years of experience in hospitality.

Shrub & Co.'s founders always enjoyed great food and wine, and eventually developed a deeper appreciation for fine spirits and the cocktail's role in a great meal. While experimenting with spirits and cocktails, Juan began reading some of the classic recipe books. One of these was Jerry Thomas's *The Bar-Tender's Guide, How to Mix Drinks (The Bon Vivant's Companion)*. Shrubs are listed as an ingredient in several recipes—which led to the question "what is a shrub?" This curiosity and home experimentation began about the same time that shrubs started popping up in cocktails at bars and restaurants. Of course, making shrubs can be labor and time intensive, which limits their use and enjoyment. Shrub & Co. decided to create shrubs made with excellent organic ingredients, fresh from local farms whenever possible.

You can order Shrub's shrubs on their website (see Resources).

The Shrub & Co. team is wild about its Peppery Peach Ice Pop, which uses 3 ounces of peach shrub, 1 teaspoon of minced Serrano pepper, and 20 ounces of coconut milk or Greek yogurt. Whisk all of that together, pour it into an ice-pop mold, and freeze it overnight for a savory and sophisticated icy treat. It makes four pops, which is probably just enough to share with a friend or three.

A THEORY OF SHRUB MAKING

I've provided nearly fifty recipes here for shrubs and more than thirty for cock-tails. You can certainly follow the shrub recipes to the letter and have a delicious product, but I urge you to think of the recipes as guidelines. When I started making shrubs, I followed the advice in recipes I found that said to use equal parts fruit, sugar, and vinegar. I was satisfied with the results, but when I started researching this book, I tweaked my formula a bit. For many of the recipes in this book, I've used roughly two parts fruit (or vegetable) to one part sugar and one part vinegar. For example, if the recipe calls for 2 cups of chopped

fruit, it then calls for 1 cup of sugar and 1 of vinegar. To me, this allows the main ingredient to shine through a little more vividly than my old 1:1:1 formula.

But that's my preference. You might have a yen for vinegar, in which case you can increase the vinegar to your tastes. Or perhaps you have a sweet tooth and you want more sugar. There are no rules, except to taste while you're mixing and take good notes so you recall what you've done.

SHOPPING FOR SHRUBBING

Ready to make some shrubs? You'll need the ingredients first: sugar, vinegar, and some combination of fruit, vegetable, herbs and/or spices. There are very few specialized tools that you'll need; a fine-meshed strainer is critical and I'll go into more depth later in this chapter with other suggestions.

I've tried to keep the recipes basic and approachable, especially since drink-ing vinegar is still a bit of a hard sell. Why list a bunch of recipes that call for hard-to-find vinegars and fruits? I really want to nurture the idea of shrub making as a way to preserve the bounty of fresh produce, alongside pickling vegetables and making jams and jellies.

Once you have played with all the things you can find in the average grocery or farmer's market, you can then branch out and try more exotic fruits and vegetables.

FRUITS AND VEGETABLES: THE MAIN INGREDIENTS!

As I've pointed out, shrubmaking started as a way to preserve citrus, berries, and other fruits, but as bartenders, chefs, and other creative drink-mixers have learned, you can make delicious shrubs from vegetables as well. The shrub recipes I've provided in the book are just the beginning—I've seen recipes for shrubs from corn to pumpkin, lychee to kumquat. If you're a person who enjoys a good farmer's market, you'll be happy to know that even the most bruised and unlikely-looking fruits and vegetables are just right for a shrub.

With that in mind, here's what to look for at the market:

BERRIES

Berries are terrific for shrubs. Raspberries, blackberries, strawberries, gooseberries, currants, and the like make the most beautiful jewel colors and mix well with soda water and many liquors. The best berries should be plump, smell fragrant, and release juice easily when you squeeze them. Choose berries that have no obvious mold on them. Mold spreads quickly on berries, so if they get moldy after you bring them home, discard the moldy berries immediately, so the mold doesn't infect the entire batch. You can also use frozen berries, just thaw them according to the package instructions.

POME FRUIT

Apples, pears, and even quince are tasty and often available year-round, although I find that apple and pear shrubs taste better when made from first-of-season fruit. If you are looking during apple and pear season, you can use "seconds," or bruised fruit. I have some tips on that a little later in the chapter. You'll know that pome fruits are good for shrubs if they are firm, crisp, and have a good color. Apples and pears both come in many varieties, but I've found that all of the common types are generally good in shrubs. I especially love using Gala, Honeycrisp, and Fuji apples in shrubmaking, though you should feel free to experiment with other varieties. Keep in mind that some varieties are sweeter than others, so you might adjust the amount of sugar up or down, depending on how sweet or tart your apples are.

STONE FRUIT

Plums, peaches, apricots, nectarines, and cherries all make for great shrubs, and they all combine well with herbs and spices to make complex flavors that shine in both sodas and cocktails. I don't always buy organic fruit for shrub-making, but stone fruit is one category where I certainly try to do so; stone fruit tend to be sprayed with pesticides more often than other crops. If you're shopping at a farmers' market, it pays to walk around and talk to the farmers before you buy. They may have "seconds" on a truck or behind the table, and you'll save money buying those. Also, if you were buying these to eat out of hand, you'd of course want a perfectly ripe fruit that will send its juices dripping down your chin. You don't need that for shrub-making, though it doesn't hurt. For shrubs, you can buy fruits that are a little harder, since you're going to hammer it with sugar and leave it in the fridge to macerate anyway.

If you're shopping at a farmers' market, it pays to walk around and talk to the farmers before you buy.

CITRUS

Unless you live in California or Florida, you're unlikely to find seasonal, local citrus fruits in your town. Now, having said that, certain varieties, such as blood oranges and Meyer lemons, are easier to find in the winter months, when citrus is in season. The most common lemon variety in supermarkets is the Eureka lemon, and that's what I used for the recipes in this book. The most common supermarket lime is the Persian, which is what I used here, but others such as Key and Kaffir limes should work for shrubs, although I've never used them. Oranges, of course, come in many different varieties, so here I can only urge you to experiment to see what you like best.

How to Make a Shrub

61

TROPICAL FRUITS

Pineapples, coconuts, papayas, and mangos all make good shrubs, either alone or in combination with other fruits and flavors. If you don't want to go through the process of peeling and cutting a fresh pineapple, you can rely on frozen; just thaw it according to the package instructions. I advise against using canned pineapple. Similarly, you can use shredded or dried coconut in shrubmaking, especially as a way to enhance or complement other flavors. Just steep it in vinegar for a day or two as you would with fresh herbs.

FRUIT VEGETABLES

This category includes tomatoes (famously a fruit, not a vegetable) as well as tomatillos, peppers, squashes, pumpkins, and cucumbers. Fruit vegetables really benefit from local, seasonal shopping, as anyone who's tasted a super-market tomato in December knows too well. Again, when you're shopping for these items, you don't need to look for peak perfection. Shop for "seconds," if your favorite farmer sells them. Experiment with heirloom varieties, but only if you like the flavor on its own. I don't find that heirloom tomatoes, for example,

Hot peppers rate a special mention. A company called Bittermens, which produces bitters and liqueurs, also makes a Hellfire Shrub, using habanero peppers, but peppers don't have to be the star of the show. Peppers can give depth of flavor to shrubs made primarily from berries, stone fruit, tomatoes, or melon, just to name a few ideas. You can steep them in the vinegar, or you can smash them up with the fruit and let the sugar extract the pepper's juice.

Ginger can be "juiced" with a grater (catch the juice as you grate), or you can slice it and steep the slices in vinegar overnight to extract their flavor. Young ginger sometimes shows up in farmers' markets and at Asian groceries. The skin is thin and doesn't require peeling, and the flesh is mildly spicy, tender, and juicy. If you're lucky enough to find some, you can make a delicious young-ginger shrub from it. Mature ginger, with the tough skin, is what you'll commonly find in the grocery. For shrubmaking, you can shred or slice it without removing the peel. When shopping for mature ginger, look for plump roots with smooth skin. You can freeze ginger for up to six months; it's actually a lot easier to grate when frozen. Immediately refreeze whatever you don't use, or it will get mushy.

are sufficiently better in shrubs to warrant the extra cost. Your standard Better Boy or Early Girl tomatoes are just fine for shrubs, though I do also love Brandywines.

VEGETABLES

Carrots, celery, and beets all make unlikely beverage ingredients, but they're all delicious in shrub sodas and cocktails. Buying locally and seasonally is helpful here because the closer to you the ingredient was grown, the fresher it's likely to taste; however, you can still make delicious shrubs from supermarket veggies you buy in December. However, with thin-skinned vegetables such as carrots, celery, and beets, it's imperative that you either buy organic or wash the produce very well before using it. Shallots, leeks, chives, and other mild-tasting alliums rate a special mention here. They can work well as secondary flavoring ingredients with vegetables and tomatoes, but be careful not to allow their flavors to run loose. I advise against using onions or garlic in shrubs, but if you try them and think they're good, drop me a line and let me know.

FRESH HERBS AND SPICES

You can use herbs and spices as secondary flavoring agents or even as the main flavor. I've heard of bartenders making mint shrubs, for example; they steep the mint in vinegar overnight. For fresh herbs and spices, I firmly suggest finding a local farmers' market. The flavors of herbs are in their essential oils, and those oils break down quickly after the herbs are harvested. Further, you want to be sure the farmers are using organic techniques to grow the herbs; you don't want to worry about pesticide residue. Just about anything is fair game in shrubmaking: Anise hyssop, basil, fresh bay leaves, bergamot zest, borage, celery leaves, chervil, cilantro, dill, fennel, horseradish, Kaffir lime leaves, lavender, lemongrass, you name it. Ginger, especially, is great in shrubs.

SECONDS

Some farmers' market stands offer "seconds," items that are not at peak market quality. Usually, these are fruits that have some bruising or bumps or small tears to the skin. Farmers sell these at a discount. Seconds are a win-win for

you and the farmer; he or she doesn't have to throw away the fruit, and seconds are perfect for shrubmaking, since you'll be crushing or chopping the fruit anyway. But still be careful. I bought a bag of peach seconds once; the fruit was so soft that, by the time I got it home, the peaches on the bottom were already crushed by the ones on top. Peach juices leaked out of the bag and all over my clothes. Look for fruit that's ripe but still somewhat firm. Small tears are fine, but some of the peaches I selected that day had bits of skin ripped off them. I should have left those behind. One of my favorite farm stands doesn't even sell peach seconds for this very reason. They're too soft to sell; the farmer feeds them to his pigs.

SUGARS AND OTHER SWEETENERS

I use basic sugars—white, cane, or turbinado—for nearly all my shrub making, for the simple reason that they're reliable. I know they work, and I have no dietary reason to avoid them. But they're not the only game in town, and you can change the flavor profile of your shrubs by trying different sugars.

Sugar has two roles in shrub making. First, it provides sweetness to the beverage and helps to balance out the tartness of the vinegar. Additionally, though, in some recipes it draws the juices out of the fruit during an overnight maceration, mingling with the juice to become syrup. For this second reason, I usually stick with granulated sugars, either white or brown, for shrubs, especially those in which I use the sugars to draw out juices. I don't generally use honey or agave nectar for shrub making, though in recipes where you're not using the sweetener to draw out fruit juice, honey and agave nectar should work fine. However, you'll probably have to adjust the quantity, either up or down, depending on your taste.

WHITE SUGARS

- **White cane sugar** is basic and easy to use. It dissolves quickly. The main downside is that is has almost no flavor of its own. Use white sugar when you really want to highlight the main flavors.

- **Raw cane sugar** is almost as versatile as white. It's a little less processed than white sugar, and therefore has just a little more of a molasses note to it. Cane sugar will also allow the main flavors to shine. It's my favorite sugar for shrub making, but it's also usually more expensive than white sugar. I like either white or raw cane sugar with main ingredients that are delicately flavored, such as stone fruit and melon.

BROWN SUGARS

Brown sugars are sugars that still have a bit of molasses clinging to them. They're richer and more flavorful than white sugars. To make them, sugar processors start by extracting cane juice from sugarcane, boiling it until all the liquid evaporates. What remains are molasses-laden crystals.

- **Turbinado** and **Demerara** sugars are quite similar to one another. Sugar makers take the molasses-laden crystals and spin them in a centrifuge (also called a "turbine," hence the name "turbinado"). The centrifuge dries the sugar and removes some of the plant material still clinging to the crystals. When tasting these, you can usually detect notes of honey or molasses, giving them a bit more richness than white sugar has. I like using both in shrubs, although only a few of my recipes directly call for one or the other. I generally like turbinado and demerara in recipes in which the fruit is already so rich and jammy that a bit of molasses is welcome—for example, cherries, plums, figs, and black currants.

- **Muscavado sugar** is not dried in a centrifuge; instead it's dried over low heat, and sometimes in the sun. The crystals retain more of the plant material; they're stickier than the other sugars and have a stronger molasses flavor. I don't find muscavado to be particularly suitable for shrub making; the flavor's a little too strong. Your experience might be different, though, so feel free to experiment.

OTHER SWEETENERS

- **Beet sugar** is a commonly available sweetener, similar to white cane sugar. I have never used it in shrub making, so I can't attest to its quality. Like cane sugar, it's 99.95 percent sucrose, but it's the other 0.05 percent that some folks say makes a huge difference. A sugar beet is a root, growing in the ground. Sugar cane is a grass, growing above ground. Each plant absorbs different minerals and proteins while growing, and some of that comes through in the flavor. Again, all I can say is, feel free to experiment. You might find you prefer beet sugar in your shrubs.

- **Maple sugar** is processed from the sap of the sugar maple tree, also the source of maple syrup. It's about twice as sweet as granulated cane sugar, and so if you use it in recipes, go with a lighter touch. I've never used it in shrub making, but I can easily see it working well with, say, apples, figs, or plums.

- **Honey** works well in shrub making, although I've never tried using it to extract the juices from fruit. In my experience, it works best when you're making cooked syrups. It's hard to combine the ingredients when you're making a cold-process shrub because honey is usually so thick. Keep in mind that honey is an animal product, and for that reason, many vegans don't eat it, so if you're a bartender or if you're offering shrubs to friends, you may want to provide a disclaimer when you're offering honey-based shrubs.

- **Agave nectar**, like honey, is also somewhat thick, so when working with it, you might want to cook your syrup so that everything mixes well.

- You can usually find **fructose sugar** in most health-food stores or online retailers. For those who need to watch their sugar consumption, this might be a good choice. In his seminal On Food and Cooking, the food scientist Harold McGee describes the properties of fructose.

> The fructose molecule exists in several different shapes when dissolved in water, and the different shapes have different effects on our sweet receptors. The sweetest shape, a six-corner ring, predominates in cold, somewhat acid solutions. . . . Fructose is thus a useful substitute for table sugar in cold drinks, where it can provide the same sweetness with half the concentration and a calorie savings approaching 50 percent. In hot coffee, however, its sweetness drops to the level of table sugar.

If the sugar level of some of these recipes concerns you, you can experiment with using fructose sugar instead and lowering the amount. However, I'd only use it in cold-process shrubs, for the reason McGee points out. In a hot-process shrub, you'd probably need the full recipe amount.

VINEGAR

French winemakers have a saying: "God loves to make vinegar." Winemaking in France dates back to Roman times, and those centuries of experience have taught vintners that it's easier to allow wine to become vinegar than it is to arrest the process and keep the wine fresh.

Vinegar captures the aromas of herbs and spices better than water, which is why I infuse the vinegar with the herb or spice in one container, while the fruit and sugar macerate together in another container.

You see, the three ingredients of vinegar are alcohol, oxygen, and bacteria. Leave wine open to the air, and natural bacteria in the air will metabolize both alcohol and oxygen and create something new: acetic acid, or vinegar. The process is so inevitable, in fact, that the food scientist Harold McGee wrote, "Vinegar is alcohol's fate, the natural sequel to an alcoholic fermentation."

The only way to prevent it is to keep oxygen away from the wine. One way to do this is by storing the wine in containers without any headspace, filling them so full that there's no room for oxygen. Another way is to use sulfites, a type of preservative that protects the wine against oxygen and bacteria.

As you can see, in a manner of speaking, making vinegar is easy. Leave a bottle of wine open on your countertop long enough, and it will turn to vinegar. The question, however, is whether that vinegar will be any good. Making vinegar might be easy. Making good vinegar? That takes some work, and I'm not going to cover it in this book.

- **Apple cider vinegar** is the workhorse of my shrub making. It's versatile, inexpensive, and easy to find, and its flavor meshes well with many fruits and some vegetables. Keep in mind that many brands, such as Bragg's, have a "mother," the cloudy-looking stuff at the bottom of the bottle. The "mother" means that the apple cider vinegar is unpasteurized. It's harmless, and some folks say it's healthy, but if the appearance turns you off, you can shake the vinegar to incorporate the mother before you use it. Alternatively, Heinz makes pasteurized cider vinegar that has no "mother."

- **Wine vinegars** tend to retain a certain amount of winey character that, I feel, make them ideal for berries and stone fruit shrubs.

- **White wine vinegar** and **champagne vinegar** are great for stone fruit, although I sometimes use apple cider vinegar for these shrubs, or a mix of the two. I find that white wine vinegar has a sharper, brighter taste than other wine vinegars, which lends itself well to delicately flavored fruits.

- **Red wine vinegar** has a jammy quality to it, which makes it ideal for berries and cherries. Again, you can use it alone or blended with other vinegars.

- **Balsamic vinegar**, I find, is generally too rich for most shrubs. There are few fruit flavors that pair well with it. Strawberries, though, are classic, and cherries work, too. Peaches are probably the only stone fruit I'd pair with balsamic. White balsamic is a little more versatile, especially with stone fruit.

- **Rice vinegar** is a distinctive choice for shrubs. Try it with carrots, ginger, pineapple, or cucumber. Because rice vinegar is less acidic than most wine vinegars, it also works as a secondary vinegar in a shrub, to temper the acid bite of the main vinegar.

- **Coconut vinegar** and **pineapple vinegar** are great for shrubs made from tropical fruits, such as mango, papaya, guava, cherimoya, kiwifruit, or lychee. Coconut vinegar also complements a shrub made from fresh pineapple.

- **Distilled white vinegar** has few uses in my kitchen, aside from pickling and cleaning. Made by fermenting distilled alcohol, distilled white vinegar is the most acidic of the vinegars, and it

Never discount the importance of a good label maker. A friend of mine recounted a story about how her peach shrub looked identical to her partner's ginger syrup, and they got mixed together in the bottle because the colors were very similar. I've had similar experiences: peach shrub looks like apricot; blackberry shrub looks like blueberry. Having to taste each shrub to remind yourself which you're tasting? Dumb. Label your bottles, whether you use tape and a marker or a portable label maker.

lacks the aromatic or savory qualities of other vinegars. I almost never use it in shrub making, although I did use a little of it in my Red Beet and Peppercorn Shrub. I used it there because I was specifically hoping to mimic the flavors of pickled beets.

TOOLS

One of the advantages of shrub making is that you don't need a lot of special tools. If your kitchen is stocked with bowls, spoons, a good knife, and a cutting board, you're in good shape. A blender can come in handy for some recipes, but you don't need to have an electric juicer. (If you happen to have one, you can certainly use it, but I didn't include recipes that require one.) In addition, you'll want:

- Citrus juicer

- Fine-meshed strainer

- Funnel

- Jars or bottles for storage (with top)

- Labels (masking tape and permanent marker work)

To use your shrubs in cocktails, you'll probably want a cocktail shaker, strainer, and jigger (or other measuring tool), but again, you don't have to go crazy stocking your bar in order to enjoy a good, shrubby drink.

PREPARING SHRUBS AND CONTAINERS FOR STORAGE

Once you've made your shrubs, the next question is, how should you store them? I'll be honest with you here; I store mine in bottles, jars, and plastic containers in the fridge. Aside from washing the containers first, I don't take any special precautions to sterilize them or otherwise prep them for service.

I will urge you to discard your shrubs after a year, on the off chance that they've spoiled in your fridge, but I'll be honest again and say, I don't always do that, either. I've used shrubs that were eighteen or more months old, and I've never suffered ill effects.

Always be sure, however, to carefully check your shrubs before serving them. Fruit and herbs are prone to attracting molds, yeasts, and other microbes. If you see mold on it, throw it away. If it's bubbling, cloudy, or slimy, it's probably fermenting, and you should throw it away. (Keep in mind, though, that some shrubs settle over time, with particulate matter settling in the bottom of the jar. That's not the same as cloudiness. Shake it well and it should be fine.)

However, if you want to be really super careful with your shrubs, I have some tips for storage that should help ensure that your shrubs stay protected from bacteria and other harmful microorganisms (see Appendix). For more information, contact your local cooperative extension agency, and ask for information about storing fruit preserves and flavored vinegars. Techniques that ensure safe storage for preserves and vinegars should work for shrubs as well.

CLASSIC & OLD-FANGLED SHRUBS

In this chapter, I present some of the first shrub recipes put into print, and provide recipes from two of the preeminent citizens of the early United States. These recipes are boozy, from an era in which shrub meant a beverage based on rum or brandy.

Speaking of rum, let's talk a little about the rums that were available when these recipes were devised. The white rums we're familiar with are filtered through charcoal to remove color and most of the flavor, and they're a fairly modern invention. The writers in this chapter would have used rums that were richer and funkier. In his book *Punch*, David Wondrich describes them as having a quality called *hogo*; the word is a corruption of a French phrase, *haut goût*, describing the "high taste" of a funky rum. Traditionally, rum had certain molasses-like aromas and flavors that may have tasted offensive when the rum was new off the still, but that mellowed out after long years in wooden barrels. Today, most of those flavors don't make it into finished rums at all.

A few, though, still do, and they have a sulfurous thump to them that gives them a character, body, and richness that work quite well in shrubs and punches.

If you can find Smith & Cross, that's a perfect choice for these recipes. Wray & Nephew White Overproof will work, too. Appleton Estate Reserve is excellent in shrubs, and might be easier to find than the others. Banks 5 Islands Blend is another great choice.

As for brandy, that's a little easier. Pick a good-quality cognac, but don't spend your lunch money on it; something like Martell will do just fine.

Benjamin Franklin's Shrub

The great Pennsylvania polymath Benjamin Franklin might never have served as president of the United States, but that's one of the few titles he never achieved in his life. Author, satirist, printer, politician, postmaster, inventor, scientist, and diplomat, Franklin was also a man of great appetite, a fellow who loved his food and drink. This recipe is adapted from one found among his papers, after he died. I've trimmed the proportions somewhat. Oranges were less sweet in old Ben's day, and so you might find that you need less sugar.

INGREDIENTS

3 large oranges, peeled and juiced (you'll need about ¾ cup juice)

1 (750ml) bottle dark rum

½ cup turbinado or demerara sugar

PROCESS

1. In a gallon-sized jar, add orange peels and dark rum. Allow peels to infuse in the rum overnight.

2. Meanwhile, combine orange juice and sugar, and allow that to set overnight so the sugar begins to dissolve into the juice.

3. The next day, remove the peels from the rum and add the sweetened juice. Seal the jar and let it sit in a cool, dark place for about 3 to 4 weeks.

ORIGINAL RECIPE

To a Gallon of Rum two Quarts of Orange Juice and two pound of Sugar—dissolve the Sugar in the Juice before you mix it with the Rum—put all together in a Cask shake it well—let it stand 3 or 4 Weeks it will be very fine fit for Bottling—when you have Bottled off the fine pass the thick thro' a Philtring Paper put into a Tunnell—that not a drop may be lost.

To obtain the flavour of the Orange Peel paire a few Oranges put it in Rum for 12 Hours—put that Rum into a Cask with the others. For Punch thought better without the Peel.

Country Gentleman's Brandy Shrub

Adapted from the second edition of *The Complete Family-Piece: And, Country Gentleman, and Farmer's Best Guide*, a 1737 manual for managing a table, hunting for wild game, and raising food in the homestead, this is one of the earliest known recipes for shrub. The author is anonymous.

INGREDIENTS

8 cups brandy

5 lemons, juiced (reserve the peels of 2 lemons)

½ whole nutmeg, grated

6 cups white wine

3 cups white sugar

PROCESS

1. Add brandy, lemon juice and peels, and nutmeg to a bottle or jar. Seal it and let it stand for three days.

2. Add wine and sugar, transferring to a larger bottle or jar if necessary. Shake well to mix it up, so the sugar dissolves.

3. Place cheesecloth into a sieve. Strain mixture through cloth, and then bottle up the liquid.

ORIGINAL RECIPE

Take 2 Quarts of Brandy, and put it in a large Bottle, and put into it the Juice of 5 Lemons, the Peels of 2, half a Nutmeg; stop it up, and let it stand three Days, and add to it three Pints of White-Wine, a pound and half of Sugar; mix it, and strain it twice through a Flannel, and bottle it up; 'tis a pretty Wine and a Cordial.

Elizabeth Cleland's Rum Shrub

From another eighteenth-century cookbook comes this recipe from Elizabeth Cleland. Her original recipe would have made over seven gallons of shrub and would have required you to buy twenty-five bottles of rum; I've taken the liberty of scaling it back. Way back.

INGREDIENTS

1 (750ml) bottle rum

1 orange, peeled and juiced (approximately 6 tablespoons juice)

2 lemons, peeled and juiced (approximately 6 tablespoons juice)

1 cup turbinado or demerara sugar

PROCESS

1. Pour rum into a one-gallon jar and add orange and lemon peels. Seal the jar and allow the peels to infuse in the rum for up to six hours or overnight.

2. Strain off the peels and return the rum to the jar. Add citrus juices and sugar. Shake well to dissolve sugar.

3. Allow this to sit for a few days until all the sugar is finally dissolved.

ORIGINAL RECIPE

Take five English Gallons of Rum, three Chopins of Orange and Lemon-juice, and four Pounds of double-refined Sugar; mix all together, but first pare the Rind of some of the Lemons and Oranges, and let them infuse in the Rum for six Hours: Let all run through a Jelly-bag, then cask it till is fine, and bottle it.

Elizabeth Moxon's Orange Shrub

~~~~~~

This recipe is adapted from a 1743 book instructing women on how to keep a proper home. It calls for Seville oranges, a variant that produces rather bitter juice that mellows nicely over time, especially when blended with lots of sugar and other citrus juices. The original recipe made a large quantity of shrub (though Moxon's made even more). The best way to peel citrus for recipes such as this is with a vegetable peeler.

~~~~~~

INGREDIENTS

18 Seville oranges, peeled and juiced

3 large lemons, peeled and juiced

2 cups brandy

1½ cups sugar

PROCESS

1. Strain orange and lemon juices through a fine-mesh sieve, and then place the juice into a large jar or plastic storage container.

2. Add brandy.

3. Add sugar to taste, and then add the citrus peels. Shake well to combine.

4. Let it stand until you're ready to drink it, or for at least three days.

5. Strain out the peels and place shrub into a bottle. With this much brandy, it shouldn't need refrigeration.

ORIGINAL RECIPE

Take seville oranges when they are full ripe, to three dozen of oranges put half a dozen of large lemons, pare them very thin, the thinner the better, squeeze the lemons and oranges together, strain the juice thro' a hair sieve, to a quart of the juice put a pound and a quarter of loaf sugar; about three dozen of oranges (if they be good) will make a quart of juice, to every quart of juice, put a gallon of brandy, put it into a little barrel with an open bung with all the chippings of your oranges, and bung it up close; when it is fine bottle it.

This is a pleasant dram, and ready for punch all the year.

Classic and Old-Fangled Shrubs

Martha Washington's Shrub

This recipe for shrub comes from a handwritten book that Martha inherited from her first mother-in-law, Frances Parke Custis. The book was handed down through the generations, originating probably in England in the early 1600s. Martha herself held onto it for 50 years, before handing it down to her grand-daughter Eleanor Parke Custis, on the occasion of Eleanor's marriage. I do not know whether history has recorded any evidence that Martha herself created this recipe or made it for anyone, but since Martha was the most famous person to inherit the cookbook, it's known these days as Martha Washington's Booke of Cookery. In 1981, a food historian named Karen Hess transcribed and annotated the manuscript for Columbia University Press. The Hess edition is still in print.

INGREDIENTS

1 (750ml) bottle cognac

1 (750ml) bottle white wine (something fairly dry, like a pinot gris)

3 cups bottled spring water

2 lemons, sliced and crushed, with the rinds left on

1½ cups turbinado or demerara sugar

PROCESS

1. Add all ingredients to a large pot, stirring well. Let it sit for several days, stirring every day, until the sugar dissolves.

2. Strain out the lemon remains using a fine-mesh strainer lined with cheesecloth.

3. Bottle it and store it, preferably in the refrigerator.

ORIGINAL RECIPE

Take one quart of brandy & a quart of white wine, & a quart of spring water. mix them together then slice 3 leamons, & put in with a pound of sugar. stir these very well, cover yr pot close, & let it stand 3 dayes, stiring it every day. then strayne it, & bottle it, & crush ye leamons very well inside it.

SWEET SHRUBS

Fruity, jammy, and full of fresh, bright flavors, sweet shrubs are a simple evocation of the height of summer and fall produce season. In this chapter, you'll find shrubs made from apples, stone fruit, berries, melons, figs, and citrus. Some are simple fruit shrubs, whereas others have herbs or spices to kick up the flavor. Bright, fresh-tasting shrubs made from apricots, currants, grapes, and various berries provide a fantastic base for fizzy, non-alcoholic sippers. You'll find recipes featuring apples and cranberries in perfect harmony; blackberries dancing with lime; cantaloupe paired with mint; and cinnamon coupling with either apples or figs.

No matter whether the main ingredient goes solo or takes a partner, these shrubs will quench your thirst on a blistering day, jazz up your cocktail repertoire, and form the basis for delightful and sophisticated sodas.

Apricot Shrub

~~~~~~

This is a simple, straightforward fruit shrub, of apricot, sugar, and vinegar. If you wanted to spice this one up, you could add cardamom, rosemary, chamomile, or lavender. To do that, you would let the apricots macerate with the sugar in one bowl, and at the same time, set a little of your herb or spice into another bowl with the vinegar, and let them steep so that the vinegar absorbs the flavor of the herb or spice.

~~~~~~

INGREDIENTS

1 pound apricots, pitted and sliced (but leave the skins on)

¾ cup sugar

¾ cup apple cider vinegar

PROCESS

1. Place apricots and sugar into a medium bowl. Mash up the apricots and stir to combine.

2. Cover bowl with plastic wrap and place in refrigerator. Allow to macerate for 1 day.

3. Position a fine-mesh strainer over a small bowl and pour the mixture through to remove the solids.

4. Combine strained syrup with vinegar. Whisk well to incorporate any undissolved sugar.

5. You may have some sugar clinging to the apricot solids in the strainer. If so, set the strainer with the solids over another small bowl. Pour the syrup-and-vinegar mixture over the solids to wash the sugar into the bowl. Repeat as needed.

6. Pour syrup-and-vinegar mixture into a clean mason jar. Cap it, shake it well to incorporate any undissolved sugar, and place in the refrigerator for a week before using.

7. Discard the solids or save them for another use.

Black Currant Shrub

One of the fun things about writing a cookbook is that you learn a lot while you're writing. One thing I never knew prior to writing this book is that black currants used be illegal to cultivate in much of the United States. It seems the bushes on which black currants grow can carry a fungus, called white pine blister rust, that is lethal to certain pine trees.

In New York State, where I live, the ban was only lifted in 2003, thanks to the development of fungus-resistant strains of currant. The musky and funky taste of black currants is excellent mixed with soda, gin, or vodka.

If you can't get black currants, you can substitute red currants.

INGREDIENTS

1½ cups black currants

¾ cup raw cane sugar

¾ cup red wine vinegar

PROCESS

1. Place black currants and sugar into a medium bowl. Crush the currants, and stir to combine.

2. Cover bowl with plastic wrap and place in refrigerator. Allow to macerate for a day.

3. Position a fine-mesh strainer over a small bowl and pour the mixture through to remove the solids.

4. Combine strained syrup with vinegar. Whisk well to incorporate any undissolved sugar.

5. You may have some sugar clinging to the currant solids in the strainer. If so, set the strainer with the solids over another small bowl. Pour the syrup-and-vinegar mixture over the solids to wash the sugar into the bowl. Repeat as needed.

6. Pour syrup-and-vinegar mixture into a clean mason jar. Cap it, shake it well to incorporate any undissolved sugar, and place in the refrigerator for a week before using.

7. Discard the solids or save them for another use.

Blackberry-Lime Shrub

I can't explain why blackberries and lime work so well together, but holy cow. If you want to add yet another flavor to this shrub, try either mint or sage (but not both). Bruise the leaves and add them along with the blackberries, lime zest, and sugar. You might need to macerate the mixture for two days to allow the herbs to give off their flavor.

INGREDIENTS

1½ cups blackberries

Zest of 4 limes

1 cup raw cane sugar

1 cup apple cider vinegar

PROCESS

1. Place blackberries, lime zest, and sugar into a medium bowl. Crush the berries, and stir to combine.

2. Cover bowl with plastic wrap and place in refrigerator. Allow to macerate for a day.

3. Position a fine-mesh strainer over a small bowl and pour the mixture through to remove the solids.

4. Combine strained syrup with vinegar. Whisk well to incorporate any undissolved sugar.

5. You may have some sugar clinging to the berry solids in the strainer. If so, set the strainer with the solids over another small bowl. Pour the syrup-and-vinegar mixture over the solids to wash the sugar into the bowl. Repeat as needed.

6. Pour syrup-and-vinegar mixture into a clean mason jar. Cap it, shake it well to incorporate any undissolved sugar, and place in the refrigerator for a week before using.

7. Discard the solids or save them for another use.

Blackberry-Raspberry Shrub

~~~~~~

This is a simple shrub, made with a combination of berries that's classic in pies
and jams. Why let those with a sweet tooth have all the fun?

~~~~~~

INGREDIENTS

1 cup blackberries

1 cup raspberries

¾ cup raw cane sugar

¾ cup red wine vinegar

PROCESS

1. Place blackberries, raspberries, and sugar into a medium bowl. Stir to combine.

2. Cover bowl with plastic wrap and place in refrigerator. Allow to macerate for a day.

3. Position a fine-mesh strainer over a small bowl and pour the mixture through to remove the solids.

4. Combine strained syrup with vinegar. Whisk well to incorporate any undissolved sugar.

5. You may have some sugar clinging to the berry solids in the strainer. If so, set the strainer with the solids over another small bowl. Pour the syrup-and-vinegar mixture over the solids to wash the sugar into the bowl. Repeat as needed.

6. Pour syrup-and-vinegar mixture into a clean mason jar. Cap it, shake it well to incorporate any undissolved sugar, and place in the refrigerator for a week before using.

7. Discard the solids or save them for another use.

Cantaloupe-Mint Shrub

Cantaloupe and mint are a very obvious pairing idea, I know. What can I say? Some ideas are simple, classic, and ubiquitous for a reason, and that reason is because they're delicious. I mean, I don't even like cantaloupe all that much, but I liked this shrub. I chose the white wine vinegar here because cantaloupe has such a delicate flavor, I didn't want a stronger vinegar to overwhelm it.

INGREDIENTS

1½ pounds cantaloupe, cut into chunks

¾ cup raw cane sugar

½ ounce mint leaves, bruised

¾ cup white wine vinegar

PROCESS

1. Add cantaloupe chunks and sugar to a bowl, stir, cover, and leave to macerate on the counter for 2 hours.

2. Meanwhile, add mint leaves to vinegar in a nonreactive container.

3. After cantaloupe has macerated, drain off the liquid and set aside. Discard the solids. Add liquid to mint and vinegar. Place in refrigerator for up to 1 week.

4. Taste until you're happy with the level of mint flavor. At that point, strain out the mint and discard the leaves.

Cherry-Mint Shrub

Of all the complementary tastes that I use in shrub, I think mint might be my favorite. It pairs well with so many different flavors.

In the case of this shrub, I used peppermint, because I specifically wanted the sharpness of the peppery herb to both complement and contrast with the sweetness of the cherries. I used a blend of vinegars because I love the bright grape flavors of red wine vinegar paired with cherries, but I also thought that cider vinegar would highlight the sweetness of the fruit.

Drink this as part of a Cherry Mint Julep, with the shrub standing in for the sugar of the original. It's also delicious with a rich, dark rum.

INGREDIENTS

2 cups sweet cherries, pitted

¼ cup peppermint leaves

½ cup turbinado sugar

¼ cup apple cider vinegar

¼ cup red wine vinegar

PROCESS

1. Place cherries, mint, and sugar into a medium bowl. Stir to combine.

2. Cover bowl with plastic wrap and place in refrigerator. Allow to macerate for 1 day.

3. Position a fine-mesh strainer over a small bowl and pour the mixture through to remove the solids.

4. Combine strained syrup with vinegars. Whisk well to incorporate any undissolved sugar.

5. You may have some sugar clinging to the cherry solids in the strainer. If so, set the strainer with the solids over another small bowl. Pour the syrup-and-vinegar mixture over the solids to wash the sugar into the bowl. Repeat as needed.

6. Pour syrup-and-vinegar mixture into a clean mason jar. Cap it, shake it well to incorporate any undissolved sugar, and place in the refrigerator for a week before using.

7. Discard the solids or save them for another use.

Cinnamon-Apple Shrub

This shrub is a simple evocation of fall, with apples, cider vinegar, and cinnamon. I used turbinado sugar here because it's a little richer than white sugar and I felt it would add a caramel note to the shrub.

If you have an urge to push this one closer to a classic apple-pie flavor, a little nutmeg in addition to the cinnamon wouldn't hurt. I would crack a whole nutmeg in half and add half a nutmeg alongside the cinnamon.

INGREDIENTS

3 medium apples, quartered (no need to core or seed them)

1 cup apple cider vinegar

½ cup turbinado sugar

2 cinnamon sticks

PROCESS

1. Using a box grater or a food processor, shred apples.

2. Add shredded apples, cider vinegar, sugar, and cinnamon to a nonreactive container. Cover and leave in cool place on the countertop for up to 2 days.

3. After 2 days, place a fine-mesh strainer over a bowl. Strain apple mixture. Squeeze or press apple mixture to remove any remaining liquid.

4. Pour liquid into clean mason jar or glass bottle. Add lid or cap and then shake well to combine. Place in refrigerator.

5. Discard solids.

6. Shrub will keep for up to 1 year.

Concord Grape Shrub

Fresh, crisp, mildly sweet, and brightly flavored, Concord Grape Shrub is a refreshing soft drink for an autumn day. It also pairs deliciously with dry vermouth, for a low-alcohol sipper. In either case, all you need is to top the drink off with soda water.

INGREDIENTS

1 pound Concord grapes, lightly mashed

½ cup sugar

½ cup apple cider vinegar

PROCESS

1. Place grapes and sugar into a medium bowl. Stir to combine.

2. Cover bowl with plastic wrap and place in refrigerator. Allow to macerate for a day.

3. Position a fine-mesh strainer over a small bowl and pour the mixture through to remove the solids.

4. Combine strained syrup with vinegar. Whisk well to incorporate any undissolved sugar.

5. You may have some sugar clinging to the grape solids in the strainer. If so, set the strainer with the solids over another small bowl. Pour the syrup-and-vinegar mixture over the solids to wash the sugar into the bowl. Repeat as needed.

6. Pour syrup-and-vinegar mixture into a clean mason jar. Cap it, shake it well to incorporate any undissolved sugar, and place in the refrigerator for a week before using.

7. Discard the solids or save them for another use.

Cranberry-Apple Shrub

Aside from pumpkin pie, fallen leaves, and football games, nothing says "fall" better than this autumnal shrub. If you're buying from a farmers' market, make the farmer happy and go for the bruised or otherwise marred fruit. You might get a discount on your purchase, and it'll save the farmer from trucking it all back home at the end of the night. And it certainly won't affect the quality of the shrub.

INGREDIENTS

3 medium apples, quartered (no need to core or seed them)

1 cup cranberries

1 cup apple cider vinegar

½ cup turbinado sugar

PROCESS

1. Using a box grater or a food processor, shred apples.

2. Meanwhile, add cranberries and vinegar to a blender. Blend until pureed.

3. Add shredded apples, cranberry-vinegar mixture, and sugar to a nonreactive container. Cover and leave in cool place on the countertop for up to 2 days.

4. After 2 days, place a fine-mesh strainer over a bowl. Strain apple-cranberry mixture. Squeeze or press to remove any remaining liquid.

5. Pour liquid into clean mason jar or glass bottle. Add lid or cap and then shake well to combine. Place in refrigerator.

6. Discard solids.

7. Shrub will keep for up to 1 year.

Elderberry Shrub

Elderberries are unusual things. The fruit is smaller than nearly any other berry. The berries come in bunches, like grapes, still clinging to their branches. But the branches are wispier than grape branches; in fact, they're almost lacy.

Unlike other fruit, nearly every part of the elderberry is toxic when eaten raw—even the fruit itself. Elderberries have a unique taste, though, so they're worth a little extra work.

INGREDIENTS

¾ cup elderberries

1 cup water

½ cup sugar

½ cup cider vinegar

NOTE

You'll want to go with a hot process here. Though I normally advocate cold-processed shrubs to keep the flavors as fresh and bright as possible, the hot process will ensure the shrub is safe. The elderberries are so pungent that cooking them won't lessen their flavor in any appreciable way.

PREPARATION

First, rinse everything really well to remove dirt and other foreign items.

Next, gently remove the berries from the branches. Hold a branch of elderberries above a bowl and then gently brush your hands back and forth against the elderberries.

Look for any green berries and discard them. Ripe berries are a deep, deep red, almost black.

Try to pick out all the woody stuff from the berries, but realize that getting rid of all of it will take crazy amounts of time. Don't go crazy; just do the best you can.

PROCESS

1. Combine elderberries, water, and sugar in a small saucepan. Set burner to medium-low and cook the mixture, stirring frequently to prevent scorching.

2. Cook until the mixture is dark red and reduced, about 15 minutes. Allow to cool.

3. Strain off and discard berry solids.

4. Add cider vinegar to berry syrup. Bottle or jar and store in refrigerator.

Sweet Shrubs

Fig-Cinnamon Shrub

Figs and cinnamon: Doesn't that just call out "fall's here!" to you? Experiment with the amount of cinnamon. I used two sticks because I wanted the cinnamon to be prominent. If you're looking for a subtler flavor, just use one. After all, you can always add more cinnamon later, if you want, but you can't take it away.

The process for this shrub differs from my normal cold process. I've tried macerating figs with sugar to extract their juices the way I do with other fruit. Doesn't work. I've tried puréeing the figs and pressing them through a sieve to squeeze the juice out. Also doesn't work.

What did work for me was to purée the figs and then infuse them, along with the cinnamon, in vinegar, and then add the sugar later, after the infusion was complete.

This shrub pairs well with bourbon or rye whiskey. I suggest mixing it into my Ditmas Park cocktail—a variation on the classic Manhattan cocktail—named for my Brooklyn neighborhood.

INGREDIENTS

1 pint purple figs, puréed in a blender

1 cup apple cider vinegar

1–2 cinnamon sticks (see headnote)

1 cup turbinado sugar

PROCESS

1. Combine puréed figs, apple cider vinegar, and cinnamon in a container. Allow to steep on the countertop for 2 days. Taste. If you started with one stick of cinnamon and you want more cinnamon flavor, add a second stick and allow to steep another day.

2. Strain off fig solids and cinnamon. Pour liquid into a bottle or jar, add turbinado sugar, and shake. Allow to sit for at least a week before using.

Gooseberry Shrub

Gooseberry. What an odd name. The name actually disguises the fact that the gooseberry is a cousin to the currant family. And perhaps the gooseberry wants to hide away from its cousins. For the gooseberry, like its cousin the black currant, is prone to white pine blister rust, the same fungus that is lethal to white pine trees. Gooseberries, like black currants, are once again legal in New York State.

Once you see them, though, grab them right away. In New York State, gooseberry plants yield fruit for only about two to three weeks.

INGREDIENTS

1½ cups (8 ounces) gooseberries, crushed

½ cup sugar

½ cup apple cider vinegar

PROCESS

1. Place gooseberries and sugar into a medium bowl. Stir to combine.

2. Cover bowl with plastic wrap and place in refrigerator. Allow to macerate for a day.

3. Position a fine-mesh strainer over a small bowl and pour the mixture through to remove the solids.

4. Combine strained syrup with vinegar. Whisk well to incorporate any undissolved sugar.

5. You may have some sugar clinging to the gooseberry solids in the strainer. If so, set the strainer with the solids over another small bowl. Pour the syrup-and-vinegar mixture over the solids to wash the sugar into the bowl. Repeat as needed.

6. Pour syrup-and-vinegar mixture into a clean mason jar. Cap it, shake it well to incorporate any undissolved sugar, and place in the refrigerator for a week before using.

7. Discard the solids or save them for another use.

Citrus shrubs use a technique that was frequently used in punch making back when punches and rum-based shrubs were common in English life. The technique was reintroduced to modern cocktail making by the booze writer David Wondrich, who discussed it in his book *Punch*. Wondrich recommends it for lemons, grapefruits, and oranges, but he says it doesn't work well with lime zest, which is too bitter for this preparation.

You make a so-called oleo-saccharum—or oily sugar, which sounds so nasty you'll surely understand why punch makers created this bastardized-Latinate term of art. The technique is actually simple.

1. Using a vegetable peeler, remove the zest of the citrus fruit in long strips. (You don't want to use the bitter white pith.)
2. Place zest into a bowl, and add sugar. Muddle sugar and citrus zest. (If you do not have a cocktail muddler, use a ladle or a wooden spoon.)
3. Cover the bowl with plastic wrap and leave alone for about an hour, or even longer if you have the time. After 1 hour (or longer), remove peels from bowl and discard, reserving the oily sugar.

The sugar will be fragrant with the smell of citrus oil, and it will add a depth of flavor to the shrub that you wouldn't get from sugar alone. You could easily adapt this technique to provide citrus aromas to other shrubs: a blueberry-lemon shrub, for example, would be lovely, using lemon oils to flavor the sugar in the shrub. (Oleo-saccharums, incidentally, also work very well for making lemonade, but that's a topic for another book.)

Grapefruit Shrub

Here's a shrub that requires a little finesse. Shrubs made from berries or stone fruits are simple to make, because it's easy to balance the three main components: fruit juice, vinegar, and sugar. Once you move into the citrus family, though, you have an added element to think about: citric acid. When citric acid meets the acetic acid in vinegar, boom! Sparks can fly. So you need to introduce them to each other nicely, and let them get to know each other a bit before leaving them in a small room together.

I always encourage shrub makers to blend according to taste, adding vinegar in small quantities to make sure you don't use too much. Here, that's imperative. Start with a mild vinegar—champagne is good. Although my recipe calls for ¾ cup, use ½ cup to start, and add more gradually, until the balance is where you like it. You might use more than ¾ cup, or you might use less.

Build an oleo-saccharum from the grapefruit peel. This adds depth of flavor. For more information on the oleo-saccharum, see page 110.

INGREDIENTS

2 large grapefruits

¾ cup turbinado sugar

¾ cup champagne vinegar (see headnote)

PROCESS

1. Zest the grapefruits and then build the oleo-saccharum using the sugar and zest, as described on page 110.

2. Juice the grapefruits. Add juice to vinegar and oleo-saccharum. Blend to combine. Add to a jar or bottle, seal it, and shake to further blend ingredients. Allow 2 to 3 days for flavors to meld.

Kiwifruit Shrub

I love kiwifruit, but I don't have it very often anymore because I'm the only one in the house who enjoys it. This shrub puts the fuzzy fruit front and center, and makes for a refreshing sparkler with soda or fizzy wine.

INGREDIENTS

1 pound kiwifruit (about 6 fruit)

1 cup sugar

1 cup apple cider vinegar

PROCESS

1. Wash and quarter the fruit. Don't bother removing the skins. Place fruit and sugar into a medium bowl. Stir to combine.

2. Cover bowl with plastic wrap and place in refrigerator. Allow to macerate for a day.

3. Position a fine-mesh strainer over a small bowl and pour the mixture through to remove the solids.

4. Combine strained syrup with vinegar. Whisk well to incorporate any undissolved sugar.

5. You may have some sugar clinging to the fruit solids in the strainer. If so, set the strainer with the solids over another small bowl. Pour the syrup-and-vinegar mixture over the solids to wash the sugar into the bowl. Repeat as needed.

6. Pour syrup-and-vinegar mixture into a clean mason jar. Cap it, shake it well to incorporate any undissolved sugar, and place in the refrigerator for a week before using.

7. Discard the solids or save them for another use.

Lemon-Lime Shrub

As with the grapefruit shrub earlier in the book, this is a shrub that requires a little finesse, so that the citric acid in the fruit doesn't clash with the acid in the vinegar.

I always encourage shrub makers to blend according to taste, adding vinegar in small quantities to make sure you don't use too much. Here, that's imperative. Start with a mild vinegar—champagne is good. Although my recipe calls for ¾ cup, use ½ cup to start, and add more gradually, until the balance is where you like it. You might use more than ¾ cup, or you might use less.

Build an oleo-saccharum from the lemon peels. (The lime peels are too bitter for this preparation.) This adds depth of flavor. For more information on the oleo-saccharum, see page 110.

INGREDIENTS

5–6 lemons (should yield about 1 cup juice)

¾ cup turbinado sugar

½ cup lime juice

¾ cup champagne vinegar (see headnote)

PROCESS

1. Remove the yellow part of the lemon peels with a vegetable peeler. Juice the lemons. Build the oleo-saccharum as described on page 110, using the sugar and lemon peels.

2. Add lemon and lime juice to vinegar and oleo-saccharum. Blend to combine. Add to a jar or bottle, seal it, and shake to further blend ingredients. Allow 2 to 3 days for flavors to meld.

Meyer Lemon Shrub

As with the grapefruit shrub earlier in the book, this is a shrub that requires a little finesse, so that the citric acid in the fruit doesn't clash with the acid in the vinegar.

Another thing to keep in mind is that Meyer lemons are sweeter than traditional lemons, and in addition to having to carefully balance the acids, you also have to balance the sugar with the sweetness in the Meyers.

I always encourage shrub makers to blend according to taste, adding vinegar in small quantities to make sure you don't use too much. Here, that's imperative. Start with a mild vinegar—champagne is good. Although my recipe calls for ¾ cup, use ½ cup to start, and add more, gradually, until the balance is where you like it. You might use more than ¾ cup, or you might use less.

Build an oleo-saccharum from the Meyer lemon peel. This adds depth of flavor. For more information on the oleo-saccharum, see page 110.

INGREDIENTS

7–8 Meyer lemons (should yield about 1½ cups juice)

½ cup turbinado sugar

¾ cup champagne vinegar (see headnote)

PROCESS

1. Remove the yellow-orange part of the Meyer lemon peels with a vegetable peeler. Juice the lemons. Build the oleo-saccharum as described on page 110, using the sugar and lemon peels.

2. Add juice to vinegar and oleo-saccharum. Blend to combine. Add to a jar or bottle, seal it, and shake to further blend ingredients. Allow 2 to 3 days for flavors to meld.

Orange Shrub

As with the grapefruit shrub earlier in the book, this is a shrub that requires a little finesse, so that the citric acid in the fruit doesn't clash with the acid in the vinegar.

Another thing to keep in mind is that oranges are generally the sweetest fruits in the citrus family, and in addition to having to carefully balance the acids, you also have to balance the sugar with the sweetness in the oranges.

I always encourage shrub makers to blend according to taste, adding vinegar in small quantities to make sure you don't use too much. Here, that's imperative. Start with a mild vinegar—champagne is good. Although my recipe calls for ¾ cup, use ½ cup to start, and add more gradually, until the balance is where you like it. You might use more than ¾ cup, or you might use less.

Build an oleo-saccharum from the orange peel. This adds depth of flavor. For more information on the oleo-saccharum, see page 110.

INGREDIENTS

5–6 medium oranges (should yield about 1½ cups juice)

½ cup turbinado sugar

¾ cup champagne vinegar (see headnote)

PROCESS

1. Remove the colored part of the orange peels with a vegetable peeler. Juice the oranges. Build the oleo-saccharum as described on page 110, using the sugar and orange peels.

2. Add juice to vinegar and oleo-saccharum. Blend to combine. Add to a jar or bottle, seal it, and shake to further blend ingredients. Allow 2 to 3 days for flavors to meld.

Peach, Ginger, and Cinnamon Shrub

Summer in a glass! Ginger pairs well with peaches because its spiciness rounds out and deepens the sweetness of the peach. The cinnamon adds warmth. I prefer white wine vinegar with peaches because of the delicacy of the fruit flavors; I find that cider vinegar is a little overbearing with peaches.

A couple of tips on the ginger: First, you don't need to peel it for this recipe. Second, I find that ginger is easier to grate when it's frozen. It also keeps for far longer in the freezer than on your countertop or in the fridge.

INGREDIENTS

6 ripe peaches (about 1½ pounds), pitted and cut into chunks

⅔ cup grated fresh ginger

1 cup sugar

1 cinnamon stick

1 cup white wine vinegar

PROCESS

1. Place peaches, grated ginger, and sugar into a medium bowl. Crush the fruit, and stir to combine.

2. Cover bowl with plastic wrap and place in refrigerator. Allow to macerate for a day.

3. Meanwhile, place cinnamon and vinegar in a nonreactive container. Allow to steep for a day.

4. Position a fine-mesh strainer over a small bowl and pour peach mixture through to remove the solids.

5. Remove cinnamon from vinegar, and add strained syrup. Whisk well to incorporate any undissolved sugar.

6. You may have some sugar clinging to the fruit solids in the strainer. If so, set the strainer with the solids over another small bowl. Pour the syrup-and-vinegar mixture over the solids to wash the sugar into the bowl. Repeat as needed.

7. Pour syrup-and-vinegar mixture into a clean mason jar. Cap it, shake it well to incorporate any undissolved sugar, and place in the refrigerator for a week before using.

8. Discard the solids or save them for another use.

Sweet Shrubs

Pear-Ginger Shrub

Here we have another classic pairing: pears and ginger. A couple of tips on the ginger: First, you don't need to peel it for this recipe. Second, I find that ginger is easier to grate when it's frozen. It also keeps for far longer in the freezer than on your countertop or in the fridge.

INGREDIENTS

6 ripe pears (about 1½ pounds), cored and cut into chunks

⅔ cup grated fresh ginger

1 cup sugar

1 cup apple cider vinegar

PROCESS

1. Place pears, grated ginger, and sugar into a medium bowl. Crush the fruit, and stir to combine.

2. Cover bowl with plastic wrap and place in refrigerator. Allow to macerate for a day.

3. Position a fine-mesh strainer over a small bowl and pour the mixture through to remove the solids.

4. Combine strained syrup with vinegar. Whisk well to incorporate any undissolved sugar.

5. You may have some sugar clinging to the fruit solids in the strainer. If so, set the strainer with the solids over another small bowl. Pour the syrup-and-vinegar mixture over the solids to wash the sugar into the bowl. Repeat as needed.

6. Pour syrup-and-vinegar mixture into a clean mason jar. Cap it, shake it well to incorporate any undissolved sugar, and place in the refrigerator for a week before using.

7. Discard the solids or save them for another use.

Pineapple Coconut Shrub

I usually stick with simple vinegars but for this recipe, I am pairing pineapple with a natural partner: coconut vinegar. You'll find it in specialty shops, natural markets, and, of course, online. As for the pineapple, fresh pineapple is best. Feel free to use cored pineapple or fresh chunks from the produce department, or buy it frozen. Steer clear of canned pineapple if you can. This is a perfect match for rum.

INGREDIENTS

4 cups cubed pineapple, crushed with your hands or a potato masher

2 cups turbinado sugar

2 cups coconut vinegar

PROCESS

1. In a bowl, combine crushed pineapple and sugar. Cover and refrigerate overnight or for up to two days, until a syrup forms.

2. Place a colander over a clean bowl. Strain pineapple mixture. Pour vinegar over pineapple solids to rinse remaining syrup through and into bowl.

3. Pour shrub into a jar or bottle. Shake well to combine. Refrigerate and store for up to a year.

HOW TO JUICE A POMEGRANATE

You don't need much in the way of equipment to juice a pomegranate. Here's what you'll need:

- A sharp knife
- A large bowl, filled with cold water
- A fine-mesh strainer and, optionally, cheesecloth
- A blender, or even a handheld fruit juicer, like the hinged types used for squeezing citrus

Your first challenge in juicing a pomegranate is getting the seed sacs (or arils) out of the fruit without also bringing the bitter pith along for the ride. Here's how you do it:

1. Take the sharp knife and cut the top of the pomegranate off, right around the crown.
2. Cut four slits partway down the sides of the fruit. Plunge the fruit and your hands into the bowl of water. Using your thumbs, pry the outer shell of the fruit apart, letting the arils and bits of pith come loose into the water.
3. Once you've pulled the fruit apart into three or four segments, start breaking the arils loose under the water. The arils are heavier than water and will sink to the bottom of the bowl. The white pith will float to the top.
4. Keep breaking the arils loose from the shell. Some will come loose in clusters with some pith attached.
5. When you're done, take a sieve and skim the surface of the water, removing the pith.
6. Drain the arils through the fine-mesh strainer. You're ready to juice!
7. Add the arils to a blender. Pulse a few times until all the arils are juiced. You might have to work in batches.
8. Drain the juice through the fine-mesh strainer (lined with cheesecloth if you want) and into the bowl.

Pomegranate Shrub

I remember the first time I tried pomegranate. I was a sophomore in college, taking a class in Greek mythology. We were reading the story of Persephone, daughter of Zeus and Demeter and queen of the underworld.

This was in Southern Indiana, and I attended college in the late 1980s, so the sight of a pomegranate was somewhat exotic, not just to me, but to my classmates as well. We were pretty astonished when the professor cut into a ripe pomegranate and passed it around the class, inviting us to taste a spoonful of the seeds, or arils.

Today, of course, pomegranate juice is everywhere, and the fruit itself is generally easy to find, from late summer into early winter. I'm providing full instructions for how to juice the pomegranates, but if you go out and buy juice, no one's going to know but you. I always suggest using fresh juice rather than bottled, and pomegranates are no exception, but I also wound up with juice all over my shirt, the countertop, the backsplash, the stove, the floor, the sink, the cats, the children . . .

INGREDIENTS

4 pomegranates (will yield about 3–3½ cups juice)

1½ cups apple cider vinegar

1½ cups sugar

PROCESS

Add all ingredients into a large bottle, and shake to combine.

Red Currant Shrub

A favorite summer drink in our household is the Vermouth Cassis, also known as the Pompier. Traditionally, this tipple is made with dry vermouth, crème de cassis (a currant liqueur), and club soda or seltzer. I wanted a shrub that could replace the crème de cassis, which I find cloying, so I wanted a less assertive vinegar here. The other advantage of white wine vinegar is that it's color-neutral, so it allows the beautiful red color of the currants to shine.

INGREDIENTS

1¾ cups (10 ounces) red currants, lightly crushed

½ cup turbinado sugar

½ cup white wine vinegar

PROCESS

1. Place currants and sugar into a medium bowl. Stir to combine.

2. You'll find that the currants are very juicy even immediately after being crushed, but a couple of hours in the refrigerator will draw out even more juice. Cover bowl with plastic wrap and place in refrigerator. Allow to macerate for 2 hours.

3. Position a fine-mesh strainer over a small bowl and pour the mixture through to remove the solids.

4. Combine strained syrup with vinegar. Whisk well to incorporate any undissolved sugar.

5. You may have some sugar clinging to the currant solids in the strainer. If so, set the strainer with the solids over another small bowl. Pour the syrup-and-vinegar mixture over the solids to wash the sugar into the bowl. Repeat as needed.

6. Pour syrup-and-vinegar mixture into a clean mason jar. Cap it, shake it well to incorporate any undissolved sugar, and place in the refrigerator for a week before using.

7. Discard the solids or save them for another use.

Rhubarb Shrub

Just for a change of pace, I want to use this recipe to demonstrate two different methods for preparing shrub: a cold process and a hot process. For the cold process, you generally macerate fruit in sugar for anywhere from about two hours to three days. The sugar draws out the juices of the fruit and makes syrup. You then strain the solids from the syrup, add the vinegar to the syrup, and mix well.

For the hot process, you make syrup on the stovetop using the fruit, sugar, and water. You add the vinegar after the syrup has cooled.

Each process has certain advantages. The biggest advantage of the cold process—and the reason I generally prefer it—is that it produces a brighter, fresher-tasting shrub. The hot process makes a shrub that has a cooked flavor; it also releases the pectin from the fruit, making a noticeably thicker syrup. The primary advantage of the hot process is that it takes less time.

I think the rhubarb shrub provides a great opportunity to try it both ways, so I'm providing recipes for both methods. For nearly every other recipe in the book, I simply provide the cold process. If you do try the rhubarb shrub both ways, I think you'll see a marked difference between the two, in terms of flavor, thickness, and color. The cold process is lighter in color and body, but richer in flavor. The hot process tastes more like a rhubarb pie (where, of course, the rhubarb is cooked), but it lacks freshness of flavor.

RHUBARB SHRUB, HOT PROCESS

INGREDIENTS

1 pound rhubarb, diced

¾ cup granulated sugar

½ cup water

½ cup white wine vinegar

PROCESS

1. Combine rhubarb, granulated sugar, and water in a small saucepan over medium-high heat, stirring as rhubarb begins to break down.

2. When mixture comes to a boil, reduce heat to low and cook until rhubarb is completely broken down into strands, about 10 minutes, stirring occasionally.

3. Remove from heat. Position a fine-mesh strainer over a small bowl, and pour the mixture through to remove the solids.

4. Allow the mixture to strain until it stops dripping, about 30 minutes. Discard the solids.

5. Allow syrup to cool to room temperature. Add vinegar.

6. Pour the resulting syrup into a jar and let cool to room temperature. Store in the refrigerator.

RHUBARB SHRUB, COLD PROCESS

INGREDIENTS

1 pound rhubarb, diced

¾ cup granulated sugar

½ cup white wine vinegar

PROCESS

1. Place rhubarb and sugar in a medium bowl and stir to combine.

2. Cover the bowl with plastic wrap and place in the fridge to macerate for 2 days.

3. Position a fine-mesh strainer over a small bowl, and pour the mixture through to remove the solids.

4. Combine strained syrup with vinegar. Whisk well to incorporate any undissolved sugar.

5. You may have some sugar clinging to the rhubarb solids in the strainer. If so, set the strainer with the solids over another small bowl. Pour the syrup-and-vinegar mixture over the solids to wash the sugar into the bowl. Repeat as needed.

6. Pour syrup-and-vinegar mixture into a clean mason jar. Cap it, shake it well to incorporate any undissolved sugar, and place in the refrigerator for a week before using.

7. Discard the solids or save them for another use.

Sweet Shrubs

Roasted Peach and Lemon Shrub

Normally when I make shrubs, I prefer to keep the base ingredient fresh and raw so it will provide the most vibrant flavors and aromas possible. In this case, though, I roasted peaches and lemons together on a sheet pan with a little simple syrup. The syrup doesn't quite caramelize, but the flavor does get deep and rich—a wonderful complement to the peaches.

Suggestions: cinnamon or nutmeg or both. Pair this with bourbon or rum in an Old-Fashioned, using the shrub to replace the drink's sugar or simple syrup component.

INGREDIENTS

5 peaches, cut in half, pits discarded

Simple syrup

4 small or 2 large lemons

1 cup turbinado sugar

1 cup apple cider vinegar

PROCESS

1. Preheat oven to 400°F. Place peaches, cut side up, on a sheet pan. Carefully pour about a teaspoon of simple syrup into the pit cavity of each peach half.

2. Cut ends off lemons and discard. Quarter lemons. Using the tip of a knife, remove as many seeds as you can and discard them. Add quartered lemons to the sheet pan.

3. Roast for 20 minutes, and remove lemons from the sheet pan. Return peaches to the oven for another 10 minutes.

4. Set a strainer over a bowl. When lemons are cool, squeeze juice through the strainer, using the strainer to catch pulp and remaining seeds.

5. When peaches are cool, transfer to a food processor and pulse until pulpy. Strain pulp through strainer into the bowl of lemon juice.

6. Add turbinado sugar and apple cider vinegar. Pour into a large bottle or jar. Shake to combine. Leave bottle or jar on counter for two days, at room temperature. Shake every few hours. When the sugar is dissolved, store in the refrigerator for up to a year.

Sour Cherry Shrub

~~~~~~

I love sour cherries. I personally think they're better than their sweeter cousins in pies, and I wanted them to star in a shrub of their own. This one works well with bourbon or rye, or just on its own. It would also be fabulous, like most fruit shrubs are, served over ice cream.

~~~~~~

INGREDIENTS

1½ cups (8 ounces) sour cherries

½ cup sugar

½ cup apple cider vinegar

PROCESS

1. Place cherries and sugar into a medium bowl. Stir to combine.

2. Cover bowl with plastic wrap and place in refrigerator. Allow to macerate for 1 day.

3. Position a fine-mesh strainer over a small bowl and pour the mixture through to remove the solids.

4. Combine strained syrup with vinegar. Whisk well to incorporate any undissolved sugar.

5. You may have some sugar clinging to the cherry solids in the strainer. If so, set the strainer with the solids over another small bowl. Pour the syrup-and-vinegar mixture over the solids to wash the sugar into the bowl. Repeat as needed.

6. Pour syrup-and-vinegar mixture into a clean mason jar. Cap it, shake it well to incorporate any undissolved sugar, and place in the refrigerator for a week before using.

7. Discard the solids or save them for another use.

Watermelon-Lime Shrub

I've already confessed my ordinary dislike of melon, but here again is another shrub that I enjoyed despite myself. The lime zest just really pops in this, adding a bright and intense citrus note to the melon flavors. This one would be spectacular with a bit of tequila and soda.

INGREDIENTS

1½ cups cubed watermelon

Zest of 1 lime

¾ cup raw cane sugar

¾ cup white wine vinegar

PROCESS

1. Place watermelon, lime zest, and sugar into a medium bowl. Stir to combine.

2. You'll find that the watermelon is very juicy even immediately after being cut up, but a day or so in the refrigerator will draw out even more juice. Cover bowl with plastic wrap and place in refrigerator. Allow to macerate for 1 day.

3. Position a fine-mesh strainer over a small bowl and pour the mixture through to remove the solids.

4. Combine strained syrup with vinegar. Whisk well to incorporate any undissolved sugar.

5. You may have some sugar clinging to the solids in the strainer. If so, set the strainer with the solids over another small bowl. Pour the syrup-and-vinegar mixture over the solids to wash the sugar into the bowl. Repeat as needed.

6. Pour syrup-and-vinegar mixture into a clean mason jar. Cap it, shake it well to incorporate any undissolved sugar, and place in the refrigerator for a week before using.

7. Discard the solids or save them for another use.

Yellow Plum and Mint Shrub

Plums and mint are almost as great together as peanut butter and chocolate. This shrub highlights both flavors very well. It would taste great with gin or even rum.

INGREDIENTS

2 cups (about 14 ounces) pitted and chopped yellow plums

¼ cup mint leaves

½ cup turbinado sugar

½ cup apple cider vinegar

PROCESS

1. Place plums, mint, and sugar into a medium bowl. Stir to combine.

2. Cover bowl with plastic wrap and place in refrigerator. Allow to macerate for 1 day.

3. Position a fine-mesh strainer over a small bowl and pour the mixture through to remove the solids.

4. Combine strained syrup with vinegar. Whisk well to incorporate any undissolved sugar.

5. You may have some sugar clinging to the plum solids in the strainer. If so, set the strainer with the solids over another small bowl. Pour the syrup-and-vinegar mixture over the solids to wash the sugar into the bowl. Repeat as needed.

6. Pour syrup-and-vinegar mixture into a clean mason jar. Cap it, shake it well to incorporate any undissolved sugar, and place in the refrigerator for a week before using.

7. Discard the solids or save them for another use.

SAVORY & SOUR SHRUBS

The shrubs in this chapter prove that you don't need to be sweetly fruity to be Mr. Popularity. Some of the shrubs in this chapter marry savory main ingredients, such as tomatoes and carrots, to spicy accents to provide a rich culinary approach to shrubs, whereas other shrubs take fruity flavors and complement them with herbs and spices you'd normally see in a kitchen spice rack. Unlikely heroes such as carrots, celery, cucumber, beets, and ginger make for rich, savory shrubs, equally delicious mixed into soda or paired with herbal liquors such as aquavit or gin. You'll also find apples paired with cardamom; berries with lavender, thyme, or peppercorn; strawberry with balsamic vinegar. These, too, make wonderful sodas as well as tasty cocktails.

Five-Pepper Shrub

This shrub was inspired by a recipe from my friend, Elizabeth Stark, who blogs as Brooklyn Supper. Elizabeth's recipe, though, is for a four-pepper jelly, not a shrub; however, I thought the mix of peppers sounded good, so I wanted to try it in a shrub. Elizabeth uses a mix of hot and sweet peppers to make a jelly with multilayered flavors—spicy-hot but still sweet.

A shrub like this would go very well in a Bloody Mary, of course, as a complement to tomato juice or tomato shrub, but it's also good with tequila and even gin or aquavit in savory cocktails.

INGREDIENTS

1 red bell pepper

1 yellow or orange bell pepper

5 jalapeño peppers

1 serrano pepper

1 poblano pepper

1⅓ cups sugar

1¼ cups apple cider vinegar

PROCESS

1. Wearing gloves, seed and chop the peppers.

2. Add peppers to a food processor and pulse until they're the consistency of finely minced garlic. You don't want a paste here, just finely chopped peppers.

3. Remove to a medium bowl, add sugar, and stir to combine.

4. Cover and place on the countertop to macerate overnight.

5. Set a fine-mesh strainer over a bowl, and strain the pepper syrup into the bowl, pressing down to squeeze all the liquid out. (You might want to wear gloves again for this.) Discard the pepper solids.

6. Add vinegar to the syrup and stir.

7. Bottle up the shrub and shake to combine. Refrigerate and store for up to a year.

Apple-Cardamom Shrub

During the summer months, not much is better than taking advantage of the simple, clean flavors of fresh produce. After all, an August tomato doesn't need much more than a little salt and olive oil—if that. But as the calendar slides into autumn, one of the joys of the colder weather is breaking into the spice rack and bringing out the warm spices. In my childhood home, that meant nutmeg, ginger, and cinnamon, but one of the pleasures of adulthood is getting to try new things. Nowadays, one of my favorite flavor pairings is apple and cardamom, and this shrub reflects that.

My recipe calls for a tablespoon of seeds, removed from the pods and lightly crushed. You can use a mortar and pestle, or even the back of a spoon. You can also use ground cardamom, but you might have to adjust the amount. Start with a teaspoon of ground cardamom and adjust according to your taste.

INGREDIENTS

3 medium apples, quartered (no need to core or seed them)

1 cup apple cider vinegar

½ cup turbinado sugar

1 tablespoon cardamom seeds, lightly crushed

PROCESS

1. Using a box grater or a food processor, shred apples.

2. Add shredded apples, cider vinegar, sugar, and cardamom to a nonreactive container. Cover and leave in cool place on the countertop for up to 2 days.

3. After 2 days, place a fine-mesh strainer over a bowl. Strain apple mixture. Squeeze or press mixture to remove any remaining liquid.

4. Pour liquid into a clean mason jar or glass bottle. Add lid or cap and then shake well to combine. Place in refrigerator.

5. Discard solids.

6. Shrub will keep for up to 1 year.

Blueberry-Lavender Shrub

I can usually smell lavender before I see it. The day I bought the lavender to develop this recipe was no exception. I was walking through the Union Square Greenmarket and caught a whiff. I looked around to find the stand that had herbs, and then finally located the lavender on a back table. Though the herb is pungent, it still complements the blueberries without being overwhelming.

INGREDIENTS

1 pint blueberries

1 cup sugar

8–10 lavender sprigs

1 cup apple cider vinegar

PROCESS

1. Place blueberries and sugar into a medium bowl. Crush the berries, and then stir to combine.

2. Cover bowl with plastic wrap and place in refrigerator. Allow to macerate for up to 2 days.

3. Meanwhile, place lavender into a nonreactive container, cover with cider vinegar, and store in a cool, dark place for up to 2 days. (The fridge is fine, but unnecessary.)

4. Position a fine-mesh strainer over a small bowl and pour blueberry mixture through to remove solids.

5. Strain vinegar mixture over the same mesh strainer, into same bowl as blueberry syrup. Allow to combine.

6. You may have some sugar clinging to the berry solids in the strainer. If so, set the strainer with the solids over another small bowl. Pour the syrup-and-vinegar mixture over the solids to wash the sugar into the bowl. Repeat as needed.

7. Pour syrup-and-vinegar mixture into a clean mason jar. Cap it, shake it well to incorporate any undissolved sugar, and place in the refrigerator for a week before using.

8. Discard the solids or save them for another use.

Carrot-Ginger Shrub

Drink your veggies! We all know why carrots are good for us; it's the beta-carotene and antioxidants and all that jazz, but ginger's good for you, too. I haven't played around much with using this shrub in cocktails. Clearly, it would work well with vodka's neutral palate. The herbaceous qualities of gin could work.

Another use for this shrub? Salad dressing! Just mix it with olive oil to your taste and add salt and pepper.

INGREDIENTS

2 pounds carrots

2 tablespoons grated ginger

1 cup apple cider vinegar

1 cup sugar

PROCESS

1. Wash carrots and, if necessary, scrub with a vegetable brush to remove dirt. Peel them if you want to, but it's not necessary.

2. Purée carrots in a blender or food processor.

3. Pour carrot purée into nonreactive container. Add grated ginger.

4. Pour cider vinegar over carrots and ginger. Stir to combine. Leave in a cool, dark place for 2 days. (The fridge is fine, but unnecessary.)

5. Place a fine-mesh strainer over another bowl. Pour carrot-and-vinegar mixture into strainer. Press or squeeze the mixture to extract all the juice.

6. Pour carrot juice into large jar. Add sugar. Cap the jar, and shake well to combine.

7. Refrigerate, shaking well every other day or so to dissolve sugar.

Celery Shrub

Celery tonic, or celery soda, is a bizarre drink and certainly an acquired taste, but those who love it can't imagine ever living without it. Dr. Brown's Cel-Ray Soda is a common fixture in Jewish delicatessens in New York City. I first encountered it at Katz's Delicatessen on the Lower East Side of Manhattan, about ten years ago. This shrub is inspired by Cel-Ray. Next time you're having a pastrami sandwich, take a bit of shrub, top it with soda, and pretend you're in New York.

INGREDIENTS

1 pound celery, leaves still attached

1 cup sugar

1 cup apple cider vinegar

PROCESS

1. Wash celery stalks and, if necessary, scrub with a vegetable brush to remove dirt.

2. Cut the stalks into 1-inch pieces.

3. Add celery to blender and cover with about 1/2 cup water.

4. Start the blender on low, and as the celery starts to get chopped up, turn the speed up to purée. If, after about 30 seconds, the mixture is still very thick and chunky, add a little more water.

5. Place a fine-mesh strainer over a bowl. Line with a piece of cheesecloth if desired. Pour the celery mixture through the strainer. Press or squeeze the celery puree to express the juice into the bowl.

6. Pour celery juice into a jar. Add sugar and cider vinegar. Cap the jar and shake to combine.

7. Refrigerate, shaking well every other day or so to dissolve sugar.

Cranberry Sauce Shrub

~~~

Here's one I did just for the fun of trying it. When my wife and I were planning our Thanksgiving dinner, we were talking about whether we wanted a traditional cranberry sauce. As we kicked around some ideas, it dawned on me that a shrub inspired by cranberry sauce would make a tasty beverage to drink before Thanksgiving dinner.

Here I use the oleo-saccharum technique described on page 110.

~~~

INGREDIENTS

1 large orange

½ cup sugar

2 cups (about 8 ounces) cranberries

1 cup apple cider vinegar

1 cinnamon stick

1 whole nutmeg, cracked

½ teaspoon allspice berries, cracked

½ tablespoon roughly chopped ginger

PROCESS

1. Build the oleo-saccharum, as described on page 110, using the orange and sugar. Using a vegetable peeler, remove the zest of the orange in long strips. Place zest into a bowl, and add sugar. Muddle sugar and orange peel. (If you do not have a cocktail muddler, use a ladle.) Cover the bowl with plastic wrap and leave alone for about an hour, or even longer, if you have the time. After 1 hour (or longer), remove peels from bowl and discard, reserving the oily sugar.

2. Juice the orange and set the juice aside.

3. Add cranberries and vinegar to a blender, and blend until puréed.

4. Add cranberry-vinegar mixture, orange juice, oleo-saccharum, cinnamon, nutmeg, allspice, and ginger to a nonreactive container. Allow to steep on the countertop for up to 2 days, so the flavors of the spices meld with the other ingredients.

5. Strain off and discard solids.

Cucumber Shrub

Perfect for pairing with gin. Splash a teaspoonful into your next martini for a subtle addition that will make your martini taste extra fantastic. I used a blend of white wine and apple cider vinegars here because I didn't want the delicate flavor of the cucumbers overwhelmed by the cider vinegar. The salt is here because I wanted this shrub to taste a little more savory than the typical fruit shrub.

INGREDIENTS

2 large cucumbers

½ cup white wine vinegar

½ cup apple cider vinegar

½ cup sugar

1 teaspoon kosher salt

PROCESS

1. Add cucumbers to blender. Blend until pureed.

2. Press puree through a fine-mesh strainer into a medium bowl.

3. Add cucumber juice, both vinegars, sugar, and kosher salt to a jar or bottle. Shake very well to combine and refrigerate.

Fennel Shrub

All about the anise, baby. Licorice, black jellybeans, absinthe, pastis, Peychaud's Bitters. If you love those things, this shrub's for you. Normally I would suggest pairing something herbal and vegetal like this with gin, vodka, or aquavit—and though those would all pair marvelously with fennel, I have another suggestion, and it might surprise you: rye whiskey. Think about the Sazerac, after all: It's a cocktail made from rye, absinthe, and Peychaud's Bitters, the latter two of which carry anise notes. Give it a shot!

INGREDIENTS

1 bulb fennel, chopped, stalks and fronds discarded

1 cup sugar

1 teaspoon fennel seeds

1 cup apple cider vinegar

PROCESS

1. Add fennel and sugar to a sealable container. Allow to macerate overnight on the countertop. Shake every so often.

2. Meanwhile, combine fennel seeds and apple cider vinegar in a container. Allow to steep overnight while the fennel and sugar macerates.

3. The next day, get in there with your hands and squeeze the chopped fennel. You can combine everything right now, or leave everything out on the counter another night.

4. When you're ready to combine the ingredients, place a strainer in a bowl. Strain crushed fennel through the strainer, and then strain the vinegar–seed mixture into the same bowl.

5. Bottle and refrigerate for up to a year.

Fresh Ginger Shrub

~~~~~~

For this shrub, I made my ginger juice the hard way. I took a couple of pieces of fresh ginger and grated them into a sieve using a Microplane grater. I then squeezed and squeezed the ginger by hand until it gave up all its juice. (I still have a scar on my knuckle from getting clumsy with the Microplane, by gum.) Puréeing the ginger in a blender or food processor and then squeezing out its juice would probably work as well and be less bloody.

~~~~~~

INGREDIENTS

½ cup ginger juice

½ cup apple cider vinegar

⅓ cup sugar

PROCESS

Combine ginger juice, apple cider vinegar, and sugar in a bottle or jar. Shake to combine.

Golden Beet and Coriander Shrub

I admit, this one seems a little unusual. Don't let that stop you; it's delicious. You want to know how I'd use it? This might seem even weirder than the shrub itself, but I'd drink it with aquavit, a Scandinavian liquor similar to gin but tasting of caraway or dill instead of juniper.

INGREDIENTS

5 golden beets, cut into small chunks

1 cup apple cider vinegar

1 cup sugar

1 teaspoon coriander seeds, crushed

1 teaspoon kosher salt

PROCESS

1. Add beets and vinegar to blender. Blend until puréed.

2. Press purée through a fine-mesh strainer into a medium bowl. You should have about 2–3 cups beet juice and vinegar.

3. Add beet-and-vinegar mixture, sugar, coriander, and kosher salt to a nonreactive container. Cover and allow to steep for 1 day. Taste. If it's not spicy enough, give it another day.

4. Place a fine-mesh strainer over a small bowl and pour mixture through to remove solids.

5. Bottle and store in refrigerator.

Plum, Peppercorn, and Bay Leaf Shrub

The inspiration for pairing plums and bay leaves came to my wife—no joke—in a dream. She suggested the peppercorns. The allspice was my idea. I started thinking about the flavors of Jamaican cuisine. Allspice is a common ingredient in Jamaican food, and my true motivation was to craft a shrub that would marry well with a rich Jamaican-style rum, such as Smith & Cross or Appleton Estate Reserve.

INGREDIENTS

1½ pounds plums, pitted and crushed

¾ cup turbinado sugar

10 black peppercorns

3 bay leaves

5 allspice berries, lightly crushed with a mortar and pestle

¾ cup apple cider vinegar

PROCESS

1. Place plums and sugar into a medium bowl. Stir to combine.

2. Cover bowl with plastic wrap and place in refrigerator. Allow to macerate for 1 day.

3. Place peppercorns, bay leaves, and allspice berries into another bowl or container. Pour on vinegar. Cover and allow to steep for 1 day.

4. Place a fine-mesh strainer over a small bowl and pour the plum-sugar mixture through to remove the solids.

5. Strain vinegar mixture over the same mesh strainer, into same bowl as plum syrup. Allow to combine.

6. You may have some sugar clinging to the plum solids in the strainer. If so, set the strainer with the solids over another small bowl. Pour the syrup-and-vinegar mixture over the solids to wash the sugar into the bowl. Repeat as needed.

7. Pour syrup-and-vinegar mixture into a clean mason jar. Cap it, shake it well to incorporate any undissolved sugar, and place in the refrigerator for a week before using.

Pumpkin Shrub

~~~~~~

Pumpkin is becoming a favorite flavor year-round, although you'll want to make this in the fall when the pumpkins are ripe. I've added a hint of cinnamon and ginger to very gently remind you of pie season, without hitting you over the head with pumpkin pie spices.

This is great served cold, either with booze (such as rum or bourbon) or on its own with soda water or, better still, ginger beer. You can also top it with hot water and your favorite brown spirit and serve it as a Pumpkin Shrub Toddy.

~~~~~~

INGREDIENTS

1 small pie pumpkin, such as sugar pumpkin or kabocha squash, about 3 pounds

1 1/2 cups turbinado sugar

1 1/2 cups apple cider vinegar

1/4 cup grated fresh ginger

1 tablespoon ground cinnamon

PROCESS

1. Adjust oven rack to center position and preheat oven to 350°F. Cut stem from pumpkin and slice pumpkin in half. Scoop and remove seeds. Place cut side down on a foil-lined rimmed sheet pan.

2. Roast pumpkin until easily pierced with a fork near the stem end, 45 minutes to an hour. Remove from oven, set aside until cool enough to handle, and then scoop out flesh with a spoon, discarding rind.

3. Add pumpkin flesh to a glass or plastic container. Add sugar, vinegar, ginger, and cinnamon. Stir to combine. Place in the refrigerator overnight or for up to 24 hours.

4. Pass pumpkin mixture through a food mill or sieve, pressing the liquid into a bowl. Mostly, you're trying to capture the liquid, a combination of pumpkin juice and vinegar, but don't worry if a little of the pumpkin purée passes through the sieve. Discard the remaining solids. Return liquid to a jar and refrigerate. Shrub will keep for several months in the refrigerator.

Raspberry-Thyme Shrub

Raspberries and thyme are common ingredients in culinary preparations, so why not in shrub? Drizzle a little of this over goat cheese for an afternoon snack, or on ice cream for dessert. This shrub also works well with olive oil in a salad dressing. Oh, you want to drink it? Try it with gin and soda on the rocks, or for a lighter touch, dry vermouth and soda.

INGREDIENTS

2 cups (10 ounces) raspberries

1 cup sugar

8 thyme sprigs

1 cup apple cider vinegar

PROCESS

1. Place raspberries and sugar into a medium bowl. Crush the berries, and then stir to combine.

2. Cover bowl with plastic wrap and place in refrigerator. Allow to macerate for up to 2 days.

3. Meanwhile, place thyme sprigs into a nonreactive container, cover with cider vinegar, and store in a cool, dark place for up to 2 days. (The fridge is fine, but unnecessary.)

4. Position a fine-mesh strainer over a small bowl and pour raspberry mixture through to remove solids.

5. Strain vinegar mixture over the same mesh strainer, into same bowl as raspberry syrup. Allow to combine.

6. You may have some sugar clinging to the berry solids in the strainer. If so, set the strainer with the solids over another small bowl. Pour the syrup-and-vinegar mixture over the solids to wash the sugar into the bowl. Repeat as needed.

7. Pour syrup-and-vinegar mixture into a clean mason jar. Cap it, shake it well to incorporate any undissolved sugar, and place in the refrigerator for a week before using.

8. Discard the solids or save them for another use.

Red Beet and Peppercorn Shrub

For this recipe, I used a mix of apple cider vinegar and distilled white vinegar. I don't normally like distilled white vinegar in shrubs, as it can overwhelm delicate berries and stone fruits. But beets are gutsy, and they can handle the stronger flavor. Further, the taste reminds me of eating from a jar of pickled beets, a fun touch.

If you have a favorite recipe for pickled beets, try adding spices from that recipe to this one. For example, if you like bay leaves and mustard seeds in your pickled beets, they'll work well in this shrub, too. Add them along with — or instead of — the peppercorns and kosher salt. Oh, and what's the salt doing there? It's just to make the recipe a little more savory.

INGREDIENTS

5 beets, cut into small chunks

½ cup apple cider vinegar

½ cup distilled white vinegar

1 cup sugar

1 teaspoon peppercorns

1 teaspoon kosher salt

PROCESS

1. Add beets and both vinegars to blender. Blend until puréed.

2. Press purée through a fine-mesh strainer into a medium bowl. You should have about 2–3 cups beet juice and vinegar.

3. Add beet-and-vinegar mixture, sugar, peppercorns, and kosher salt to a nonreactive container. Cover and allow to steep for 1 day. Taste. If it's not peppery enough, give it another day.

4. Place a fine-mesh strainer over a small bowl and pour mixture through to remove solids.

5. Bottle and store in refrigerator.

Strawberry Balsamic Vinegar Shrub

Some flavor combinations are just too obvious for me to pass up, and the classic pairing of strawberries and balsamic vinegar is one of them. You'll do well to use a good, honest balsamic vinegar here, but don't go crazy buying the super-aged stuff.

INGREDIENTS

1½ cups (8 ounces) strawberries, hulled and quartered

½ cup sugar

½ cup balsamic vinegar

PROCESS

1. Place strawberries and sugar into a medium bowl. Stir to combine.

2. Cover bowl with plastic wrap and place in refrigerator. Allow to macerate for at least 2 hours or up to a day.

3. Position a fine-mesh strainer over a small bowl and pour the mixture through to remove the solids.

4. Combine strained syrup with vinegar. Whisk well to incorporate any undissolved sugar.

5. You may have some sugar clinging to the strawberry solids in the strainer. If so, set the strainer with the solids over another small bowl. Pour the syrup-and-vinegar mixture over the solids to wash the sugar into the bowl. Repeat as needed.

6. Pour syrup-and-vinegar mixture into a clean mason jar. Cap it, shake it well to incorporate any undissolved sugar, and place in the refrigerator for a week before using.

7. Discard the solids or save them for another use.

Savory and Sour Shrubs

167

Strawberry-Peppercorn Shrub

The pepper in this shrub might surprise you. On your first sip, the main flavor is strawberry, but as you swallow the shrub, the pepper startles the back of your tongue and lingers, subtly, on the finish. If you're not afraid of a bit of mild heat, this is an enchanting drink.

I suggest pairing this one simply with soda water, although adding tequila to this particular shrub and soda would be delicious as well.

INGREDIENTS

1½ cups (8 ounces) strawberries, hulled and quartered

½ cup sugar

2 teaspoons coarsely ground black pepper

1 cup apple cider vinegar

PROCESS

1. Place strawberries, sugar, and pepper into a large jar. Tighten lid, and then shake to combine.

2. Place in refrigerator. Allow to macerate for at least 2 hours and up to 1 day.

3. Add vinegar, tighten lid, shake, and return to fridge for an additional 2 days.

4. Position a fine-mesh strainer over a small bowl and pour the mixture through to remove the solids.

5. Combine strained syrup with vinegar. Whisk well to incorporate any undissolved sugar.

6. Pour syrup-and-vinegar mixture into a clean mason jar. Cap it, shake it well to incorporate any undissolved sugar, and place in the refrigerator for a week before using.

Summer Tomato and Celery Shrub

I came up with this shrub to complement or even replace the tomato juice in a Bloody Mary (shown here). I used Brandywines for two reasons: I love them and also because they were plentiful at the farmers' market when I was shopping. Any peak-season tomato should work just as well in this recipe, though, so choose the freshest tomatoes you can find.

INGREDIENTS

2 pounds Brandywine tomatoes, cored and cut into eighths

1 tablespoon kosher salt

1 cup turbinado sugar

1 cup celery leaves, chopped and bruised

1 cup apple cider vinegar

PROCESS

1. Combine tomatoes, salt, and sugar in a nonreactive container. Crush the tomatoes with your hands to squeeze out the juice. Seal container and place in fridge overnight.

2. Meanwhile, in a separate nonreactive container, combine celery leaves and apple cider vinegar. Seal container and leave in a cool, dry place overnight.

3. Strain and reserve tomato juice. Strain and reserve celery-flavored vinegar. Combine liquids in a bottle. Discard solids.

Sungold Tomato and Basil Shrub

Sungold tomatoes are a hybrid variety of cherry tomato developed in Japan, by the Tokita Seed Company. The fruit has a gold-orange color and a sweet-tart flavor that makes it a natural for shrub. In this recipe, I paired them with apple cider vinegar and peppery basil. Sungold tomatoes should be easy to find, but if you can't locate them, you can substitute other tomatoes.

I wanted to capture the basil's essential oils at the peak of their freshness, so I infused the vinegar with the basil at the same time I started macerating the tomatoes. I didn't want even a single day to pass before I captured the flavor of the basil. If you want to skip this step, simply add the basil and vinegar to the macerated tomatoes after the second day and place back into the refrigerator for one week.

INGREDIENTS

1 pound Sungold tomatoes, halved

½ cup turbinado sugar

15–20 basil leaves (about ½ ounce), bruised

½ cup apple cider vinegar

NOTE

To bruise basil, simply place one leaf in the palm of your hand. With your other hand, sharply slap the leaf. This releases the essential oils trapped in the cells of the leaf.

PROCESS

1. Place tomatoes and sugar into a bowl. Stir to combine. Cover with plastic wrap and store in fridge for up to 2 days.

2. Meanwhile, place basil leaves into a nonreactive container, cover with cider vinegar, and store in a cool, dark place for up to 2 days.

3. Combine the tomato-sugar mixture, any accumulated liquid, and the basil-vinegar mixture in a large glass jar. Lid it up and shake it well to combine. Return to fridge for 1 week.

4. After 1 week, strain off the solids, reserving the liquid. Discard the solids. Bottle the liquid.

Tomatillo Shrub

~~~~~~

A gorgeous shrub for summer, this one has all the bright citrus notes of peak-season tomatillos. For a change of pace, try this in place of tomato juice (or tomato shrub) in a Bloody Mary.

~~~~~~

INGREDIENTS

1 pound tomatillos, hulled and quartered (or about 1 cup juice)

½ cup apple cider vinegar

½ cup sugar

1 teaspoon kosher salt

PROCESS

1. Purée tomatillos in blender until smooth.

2. Press purée through a fine-mesh strainer into a medium bowl. You should have about 1 cup tomatillo juice.

3. Combine tomatillo juice, apple cider vinegar, sugar, and salt in a nonreactive container. Seal it all up and give it a good shake. Refrigerate.

Tomato, Cilantro, and Coriander Shrub

Summertime, and the shrubbin' is easy. Options abound at groceries, farm stands, farmers' markets, and maybe your own backyard. Tomatoes are a perfect choice, and why not spice them up a little?

Cilantro and coriander are products of the same herb, Coriandrum sativum. North Americans generally use cilantro to describe the leaves and coriander to describe the seeds. If you're among those for whom cilantro reminds you of soap, feel free to swap in other peak-of-summer herbs. Basil would be lovely. Tarragon would be nice. Dill? Of course.

Or, if you love cilantro like I do, you could easily drive this shrub down Salsa Highway, and add chopped peppers and onions to the vinegar, along with the leaves and seeds.

Curious about the salt? I wanted it to draw more of the juices from the tomatoes than the sugar would do alone. Since I mean for this to be a savory shrub, I didn't think the salt would affect the flavor. Please do be sure to grind your own coriander for this, rather than using pre-ground. The flavor's better.

INGREDIENTS

2 pounds tomatoes, cored and quartered

1 tablespoon kosher salt

1 cup turbinado sugar

½ cup cilantro leaves, torn and bruised

1 teaspoon whole coriander, ground with a mortar and pestle or spice grinder

1 cup apple cider vinegar

PROCESS

1. Place tomatoes, salt, and sugar into a bowl. Stir to combine. Cover with plastic wrap and store in fridge for up to 2 days.

2. Meanwhile, place cilantro leaves and ground coriander into a nonreactive container, cover with vinegar, and store in a cool, dark place for up to 2 days.

3. Position a fine-mesh strainer over a small bowl and pour the tomato-sugar mixture through to remove the solids.

4. Strain the vinegar to remove the solids.

5. Combine strained syrup with flavored vinegar. Whisk well to incorporate any undissolved sugar.

6. You may have some sugar clinging to the solids in the strainer. If so, set the strainer with the solids over another small bowl. Pour the syrup-and-vinegar mixture over the solids to wash the sugar into the bowl. Repeat as needed.

7. Pour syrup-and-vinegar mixture into a clean mason jar. Cap it, shake it well to incorporate any undissolved sugar, and place in the refrigerator for a week before using.

8. Discard the solids or save them for another use.

Watermelon-Basil Shrub

Confession time: I don't like watermelon, or really any melon at all. I don't know why, exactly. Melons are always very juicy, which is a quality I like in fruit. And I can understand and appreciate why so many people go gaga over watermelon every summer, when the juicy fruit is so refreshing. But there's just something about the flavor of melons that I can't embrace.

Nevertheless, even I liked this shrub. Watermelon and basil are frequent salad partners, so I thought they'd work well together here, too. My wife, who *loves* watermelon, drank our entire stock of this shrub in about two weeks.

INGREDIENTS

1½ cups cubed watermelon

¾ cup raw cane sugar

15–20 basil leaves (about ½ ounce), bruised

¾ cup white wine vinegar

PROCESS

1. Place watermelon and sugar into a bowl. Stir to combine. Cover with plastic wrap and store in fridge for up to 2 days.

2. Meanwhile, place basil leaves into a nonreactive container, cover with vinegar, and store in a cool, dark place for up to 2 days.

3. Position a fine-mesh strainer over a small bowl and pour the watermelon-sugar mixture through to remove the solids.

4. Strain vinegar mixture over the same mesh strainer, into same bowl as watermelon syrup. Allow to combine.

5. You may have some sugar clinging to the solids in the strainer. If so, set the strainer with the solids over another small bowl. Pour the syrup-and-vinegar mixture over the solids to wash the sugar into the bowl. Repeat as needed.

6. Pour syrup-and-vinegar mixture into a clean mason jar. Cap it, shake it well to incorporate any undissolved sugar, and place in the refrigerator for a week before using.

7. Discard the solids or save them for another use.

ORIGINAL COCKTAILS & SOPHISTICATED SODAS

This chapter features some of my own original creations, as well as drinks from bars and restaurants around the country. You'll find cocktails that feature shrubs made from cranberries, cucumber, pomegranate, plums, apples, strawberries, ginger, and figs. I also provide recipes for sodas using celery, lemon-lime, and ginger shrubs. There's even a shrubby twist on the ice-cream float in this chapter!

Shrubs provide a nice array of flavors that work very well in cocktails and sodas, and you can find them on the menu at bars and restaurants across the country. Look around, and you'll find cocktails based on such intriguing flavors as pumpkin, apple, and tarragon; or blackberry, beet, and sage.

Sodas, too, reward creative use of shrubs: nearly any shrub will pair well with soda water to create a simple cocktail, but you can also blend shrubs with juices or flavored syrups to make something more complex. Orgeat (an almond syrup) is especially good with lemon-lime, ginger, or berry shrubs. When creating mocktails, combine something tart (shrub!) with something sweet (maple syrup or flavored syrup) and something with body, such as juice, sparkling water, or non-alcoholic wine. Experiment and have fun!

Bee Royalty

Charlie Crebs created this cocktail for Gather Restaurant, located in downtown Berkely, CA. He starts with Shrub and Co.'s Spicy Ginger Shrub, which adds a wonderful tart complexity to drinks. The base is a dry gin, in this case by City of London, which adds a wonderful balance of juniper and citrus.

Crebs likes to incorporate wine into his cocktails, and here he uses Müller-Thurgau, which adds wonderful minerality and bright acidity. He rounds out the drink with syrup made from locally-sourced orange blossom honey.

INGREDIENTS

1½ ounces City of London Gin

¾ ounce Shrub & Co.'s Spicy Ginger Shrub

½ ounce dry Riesling

½ ounce Honey Syrup

½ ounce Lemon Juice

PROCESS

1. Add all ingredients into a cocktail shaker, add ice and shake

2. Double strain into a coupe glass.

NOTE

To make the honey syrup, put equal amounts of water and honey in a small saucepan. Bring to a boil and swirl to dissolve the honey. Cool before using.

Cinderella's Carriage

A cocktail perfect for a chilly autumn night, this one combines a strong apple brandy with pumpkin shrub and rich allspice liqueur.

INGREDIENTS

2 ounces apple brandy (I like the 100-proof bottling of Laird's)

½ ounce Pumpkin Shrub (page 160)

¼ ounce allspice liqueur

Nutmeg, for garnish

PROCESS

1. Add ingredients to an ice-filled cocktail shaker. Shake hard until very cold and somewhat diluted.

2. Strain into a chilled cocktail glass.

3. Grate nutmeg over the top.

Dr. Mike's Celery Tonic

I have to admit, this is a simple recipe, even by my own lazy standards. Try this with a pastrami sandwich or a large kosher hot dog, and pretend you're at Katz's Delicatessen in New York . If you want to add some booze, go for it. Vodka's okay, but it won't add much flavor. Gin is better. Dry (white) vermouth might be even better still.

INGREDIENTS

2 ounces Celery Shrub

½ ounce Lemon-Lime Shrub

PROCESS

Combine both shrubs in an ice-filled highball glass. Add booze if using. Top with soda and gently stir.

Garland

Named for the garlands of cranberries that people sometimes use to decorate Christmas trees, this cocktail calls for gin, cranberry shrub, and sloe gin. I developed it on Thanksgiving 2013, when a friend of ours was visiting for dinner and wanted a festive pre-dinner cocktail. Sloe gin is a British liqueur made from infusing sloe berries in gin. It's fruity and only mildly sweet. It's sometimes hard to find a good sloe gin, so look for the bottling made by Plymouth. I'd go for a classic London dry gin for this recipe; the heavy juniper notes will remind you of pine, which will remind you of Christmas.

INGREDIENTS

2 ounces gin

1 ounce Cranberry Sauce Shrub

½ ounce sloe gin

PROCESS

1. Add ingredients to an ice-filled cocktail shaker. Shake hard until very cold and somewhat diluted.

2. Strain into a chilled cocktail glass or serve with single large ice cube

Gin Genie

With a name inspired by a David Bowie song, this cocktail just sprang into my mind one afternoon while I was trying to decide what I wanted to drink that evening. I initially mixed it without the Grand Marnier, but I found it to be a little too dry. I think you could probably swap out the Grand Marnier and instead use some Yellow Chartreuse in this drink; the herbal complexity of the Chartreuse would probably be quite nice with this cocktail.

INGREDIENTS

2 ounces London dry gin

¾ ounce Fresh Ginger Shrub

¾ ounce Lemon-Lime Shrub

½ ounce Grand Marnier

Crystalized ginger, for garnish

PROCESS

1. Add all ingredients except garnish to an ice-filled cocktail shaker. Shake well.

2. Strain into a chilled cocktail glass or serve over ice. Add garnish.

Lemon-Lime Rickey

A Rickey is a highball cocktail invented in Washington, D.C., in the 1880s, during a hot Potomac River summer. The original Rickey called for bourbon, apparently, but it's more common these days to use gin. However, there's a variation on the Gin Rickey that became popular during the days of the soda fountain, and that's a non-alcoholic version. A virgin Lime Rickey is a great homemade drink to serve to kids in the summer, especially if you don't want them drinking commercial soft drinks.

Mine is a simple mix of lemon-lime shrub and soda water, although you can really use any of the fruity shrubs in this. Likewise, you can blend shrubs: lemon-lime and sour cherry would be lovely, for example. If you want to drink like a nineteenth-century big shot, you can certainly add bourbon or gin. Just don't let the kids get that one.

INGREDIENTS

2 ounces Lemon-Lime Shrub (page 114)

Soda water

PROCESS

Add shrub and soda to an ice-filled glass. Stir gently to blend.

Paraíso

Trust me on this one; this is a delicious cocktail. The tequila and strawberry pairing is the backbone of this drink. (If you've never had tequila and strawberries together, you're going to be surprised by how deliciously they pair up.) The Campari gives a note of herbal bitterness that highlights the grassy notes in the tequila, while the citrus from the Cointreau and the lemon juice complements the other flavors. I'm pretty adamant about the Cointreau in this. I tried it with Grand Marnier, and the drink was a little too dry, but I can guarantee that if you use cheap triple sec, it'll be too sweet. Cointreau adds just the right level of sweetness.

INGREDIENTS

1½ ounces tequila

¾ ounce Strawberry-Peppercorn Shrub (page 168)

½ ounce Campari

½ ounce Cointreau

½ ounce lemon juice

PROCESS

1. Add all ingredients to an ice-filled cocktail shaker. Shake hard until the ingredients combine and the drink is diluted.

2. Strain into a chilled cocktail glass.

Queen of the Underworld

Named for Persephone, a character from Greek mythology. The daughter of Zeus and the harvest goddess Demeter, Persephone was abducted by Hades, king of the underworld, and became his wife. She's often shown in Greek art holding a pomegranate.

INGREDIENTS

1¾ ounces reposado tequila

¾ ounce Pomegranate Shrub (page 127)

¼ ounce lime juice

Lime wheel, for garnish

PROCESS

1. Add all ingredients but garnish to an ice-filled cocktail shaker. Shake hard to blend the ingredients and dilute the cocktail.

2. Strain into a chilled cocktail glass and add garnish.

Shallow Grave

This one pairs gin with apple-cardamom shrub. Juniper, lemon, and cardamom are ingredients that always play nicely together, so this was an easy combination to come up with. Pimm's is an English liqueur, a fruit cup made with
a blend of fruit, herbs, spices, and gin.

INGREDIENTS

2 ounces gin

**1 ounce Apple-Cardamom
Shrub (page 143)**

½ ounce lemon juice

½ ounce Pimm's No. 1 Cup

PROCESS

1. Add ingredients to an ice-filled cocktail shaker. Shake hard to
    blend ingredients and dilute the cocktail.

2. Strain into a chilled cocktail glass.

Shirley Temple

~~~~~~

I would be remiss to exclude the classic virgin cocktail, perhaps the first adult-type beverage many of us ever try. The original, of course, is either ginger ale or lemon-lime soda with a splash of grenadine. If you order it in most restaurants or bars, you'll get a cheap premixed grenadine that's nothing more than corn syrup mixed with artificial color and flavor. Gross. True grenadine is little more than pomegranate syrup, but why bother with that when we have shrub?

Add booze to this (gin or vodka, traditionally), and you have a Shirley Temple Black.

~~~~~~

INGREDIENTS

1 ounce **Lemon-Lime Shrub** (page 114)

1 ounce **Fresh Ginger Shrub** (page 157)

¼ ounce **Pomegranate Shrub** (page 127)

PROCESS

Add all shrubs to a highball glass and stir. Add soda water and gently stir again. Add garnish.

Shrub Float

Here's a soda that all ages can enjoy. This one hearkens back to the old days of the soda fountain or the ice-cream parlor. You can use any of the sweet shrubs for this one; we tested the concept twice, once with cherry-mint shrub and once with pomegranate. Have lots of fun with the frozen part of it, too. Black cherry with chocolate ice cream would be fantastic. Pomegranate with lime sherbet would be great, too. Or try an apple shrub and vanilla ice cream, but use ginger ale instead of soda water. Want a creamsicle-inspired float? How about orange shrub and vanilla ice cream?

Want to booze it up? An ounce of rum or bourbon wouldn't hurt, or add a bit of some sort of fruit liqueur or cordial: a bit of Grand Marnier or Pimm's No. 1 Cup. Really, this float isn't so much a recipe as it is a template for exciting summer refreshment. Have some fun!

INGREDIENTS

2 scoops ice cream, sorbet, sherbet, or other frozen dessert

2 ounces sweet, fruity shrub, such as Cherry-Mint Shrub (page 96) or Orange Shrub (page 119)

1 ounce rum, bourbon, Grand Marnier, Pimm's, or other liquor or liqueur (optional)

Soda water

PROCESS

1. In a float glass or other large tumbler, add ice cream, shrub, and liquor or liqueur, if using.

2. Top with soda water and stir. Serve with a straw.

Sing Sing Death House

Niklas Morris, a bartender at Scott & Co. in Tucson, Arizona, contributed this cocktail, He found inspiration in an album of the same name by the punk band The Distillers. The cocktail blends apple brandy with the herbal punch of gin. Two sophisticated and complex ingredients round out the drink. The first is Citron Sauvage, a bitter grapefruit liqueur from the bitters company Bittermens. The other one is Peychaud's Bitters, a brand of bitters that arose in New Orleans and has a hint of anise and other herbs.

INGREDIENTS

1 ounce apple brandy

1 ounce New American Gin (St. George Terroir)

½ ounce Apple-Cardamom Shrub (page 143)

½ ounce lemon juice

¼ ounce grenadine

¼ ounce Bittermens Citron Sauvage

5 dashes Peychaud's Bitters

PROCESS

1. Add all ingredients except for garnish to an ice-filled cocktail shaker. Shake until well mixed.

2. Strain into old-fashioned glass.

NOTE

You can use the Cinnamon-Apple Shrub for this, purchase a premade apple shrub, or make the Cinnamon-Apple, but leave out the spice.

Transoceanic Cooler

~~~~~~

This sparkling, low-alcohol sipper is a perfect drink for hot summer days. Crisp and refreshing, with the Pineapple Coconut Shrub, it provides a subtle nod to tropical libations.

~~~~~~

INGREDIENTS

1½ ounces Amontillado sherry

¾ ounce red Italian vermouth

¾ ounce Pineapple Coconut Shrub (page 125)

2 dashes Angostura bitters

Sparkling water

PROCESS

1. In a highball glass, stir sherry, vermouth, shrub, and bitters. Top with sparking water and stir again to combine.

HOMEMADE VINEGARS

The Velvet Tango Room, a cocktail bar in Cleveland, Ohio, put shrubby cocktails on its menu in the summer of 2013. The vinegar in its shrubs comes from the chef of Cleveland's Greenhouse Tavern. Jonathon Sawyer used to start his homemade vinegar in the stone-walled cellar of his home, using leftover wine, beer, and cider from Greenhouse and his other restaurants. Now, though, he partners with an Ohio distillery for the production work. He ages the liquid until it ferments, using a mother that he carefully nurtures. Flavors include Lemon and Beer Vinegar, Garlic Vinegar, Winter Ale, Doppel Bock, Rosé Wine, Stout Beer, Chardonnay, and Riesling.

Velvet Tango Room's Fig Shrub Cocktail

Claudia Young created this cocktail for the Velvet Tango Room, a cocktail lounge in Cleveland, Ohio. She starts with a house-made fig shrub, made of Turkish figs, brown sugar, and a red wine vinegar made by Cleveland chef Jonathon Sawyer. This drink has scotch in it, Johnnie Walker Red, but not too much. The idea isn't to create a particularly boozy drink; the scotch is just there for nuance.

Cocchi Americano Rosa is a sweet Italian vermouth; it's aromatic and lush, and it tastes quite good served simply, over ice with soda. Cocchi is distributed by Haus Alpenz, and it's available in over forty states now. You might need to call around, but you should be able to find it. It's worth a little legwork.

Be careful with the dry curaçao. You don't want to buy anything too sweet, or it will overwhelm the drink. I like the bottling made by Pierre Ferrand, a cognac maker. Ferrand's is very dry and bright with the flavor of bitter orange peel. If you can't find Ferrand's, Cointreau is an acceptable substitute.

INGREDIENTS

1¾ ounces Fig-Cinnamon Shrub (page 106)

1¾ ounces Cocchi Americano Rosa

1 ounce dry curaçao

1 tablespoon Johnnie Walker Red

Orange wheel, for garnish

PROCESS

1. Add all ingredients except for garnish to an ice-filled cocktail shaker. Shake until well mixed.

2. Strain into old-fashioned glass with three ice cubes, and garnish with orange wheel.

NOTE

You can use the Fig-Cinnamon Shrub for this, purchase a premade fig shrub, or make the Fig-Cinnamon, but leave out the spice.

Velvet Tango Room's Peach Shrub Cocktail

Claudia Young created this cocktail for the Velvet Tango Room, a cocktail lounge in Cleveland, Ohio. She starts with a house-made peach shrub, made of peaches, white sugar, and double-oaked Chardonnay vinegar made by Cleveland chef Jonathon Sawyer. This cocktail is bright, fizzy, and festive.

INGREDIENTS

1¾ ounces Peach, Ginger, and Cinnamon Shrub (page 121)

½ ounce Yellow Chartreuse

3–4 ounces Champagne

PROCESS

1. Add shrub and Chartreuse to an ice-filled cocktail shaker. Stir until chilled.

2. Strain into a champagne flute, and top with champagne.

NOTE

You can use the Peach, Ginger, and Cinnamon Shrub for this, purchase a premade peach shrub, or make the Peach, Ginger, and Cinnamon Shrub, but leave out the ginger and cinnamon.

UPDATED CLASSICS

The classics. They're drinks that have been around for decades, if not longer, and when they're well made, they're always delicious and relaxing.

I don't exactly feel comfortable saying that my shrubby additions to the classics improve them, necessarily. Take, for example, the Aquabeet Martini that kicks this chapter off. I think it's delicious, and I hope you will, too, but I also think a classic gin martini is equally delicious.

At any rate, here you'll find variations on such drinks as the martini, mint julep, cosmopolitan, Manhattan, gimlet, Gin Daisy, Kir Royale, Vermouth Cassis, sangrita, Negroni, toddy, old-fashioned, and Southside, among others.

There's another group of drinks that lend themselves very well to shrubs, and those are the ones in which the non-alcoholic portion of the drink carries a little extra flavor. These are drinks where the non-boozy modifier is based on fruity or spicy flavors, and those are perfect for shrubs. These include the Campari Soda, Greyhound, Moscow Mule, Dark 'n Stormy, and Bloody Mary, among others.

Aquabeet Martini

I hate cocktails that are called "martini" but don't resemble a classic martini in any way. I also hate the trend of attaching "-tini" to an overly sweet concoction of schnapps, vodka, and gummy bears or whatever.

This cocktail is very much in the model of a classic martini. In place of gin, I call for aquavit, a caraway-infused vodka from Scandinavia. I call for vermouth because I think it's absolutely necessary for a true martini, though I don't call for much of it. The ratio is 10 parts aquavit to 1 part vermouth, which is pretty dry as these things go. (The original martini was equal parts gin and vermouth.) Finally, I polish it off with a spicy beet shrub. If you want to amuse your guests, you might garnish with a very thin slice of beet, floated gently atop the cocktail. But since so many people are anti-beet, you'll have to use caution with this approach.

INGREDIENTS

2½ ounces aquavit

¼ ounce dry vermouth

¾ ounce Golden Beet and Coriander Shrub (page 158)

PROCESS

1. Add ingredients to a mixing glass halfway full of ice.

2. Stir for 30 seconds.

3. Strain into chilled glass.

Campari Soda

The Campari Soda is a popular Italian aperitif, served in cafés throughout the country. Campari even markets a pre-bottled version of the drink, which you can just crack open and sip from the bottle. I like to take another Italian beverage, San Pellegrino, and mix that with Campari. San Pellegrino also makes several fruit sodas—Limonata (lemon soda), Aranciata (orange soda), Rosso Aranciata (blood-orange soda), and Pompelmo (grapefruit soda).

As nice as this is, though, there's no reason you can't do it on your own with shrub. Take a lemon, orange, blood orange, or grapefruit shrub. Add Campari, and top it off with soda water. If you want to use a soda with some minerality, like San Pellegrino, go for it.

INGREDIENTS

2 ounces Campari

1 ounce fruit shrub of your choice

Soda water

PROCESS

Fill a tall, narrow glass with ice. Add Campari and shrub. Top with soda water.

Cherry-Mint Julep

Here's a traditional julep recipe, but one in which I've replaced the sugar (or simple syrup) of the original with cherry-mint shrub.

I suggest starting with a high-proof bourbon or rye, something over 90 proof (45 percent alcohol by volume). Why? Well, think of how you drink a julep. You serve it over crushed ice and sip it slowly. Over time, the ice melts into the drink, chilling it down so it's very cold. But melting brings dilution. The higher the proof of your spirit, the less watery your drink will taste at the end.

A note on muddling mint: You want to lightly bruise the mint, to release its oils into the glass. If you vigorously crush the mint, you break open the veins of chlorophyll that run through the leaves. Chlorophyll is bitter, as you probably know if you've ever eaten a mint leaf. So when you're muddling, press lightly on the mint. Any amount of pressure will release the oils, so be gentle.

INGREDIENTS

2 teaspoons Cherry-Mint Shrub (page 96)

8–10 fresh mint leaves

2–3 ounces high-proof bourbon or rye, to taste

Mint sprigs, for garnish

PROCESS

1. Place shrub at the bottom of a julep cup or tall glass. Add mint leaves and gently bruise with a wooden muddler or a wooden spoon. Be sure to swab the sides of the glass with the mint's aromatic oils.

2. Half-fill the glass with crushed ice and add the bourbon or rye, stirring to combine. Fill the glass with crushed ice and stir until the outside of the glass frosts. Add more crushed ice if needed to fill the glass. Garnish with a generous amount of fresh mint. The aromas of the mint garnish are part of the experience.

Desmond Daiquiri

This cocktail, named after the ska and reggae pioneer Desmond Dekker, features rich Jamaican-style rum, my spicy plum shrub, and lime juice. Jamaican rum is a style of rum that is rich, fruity, and flavorful, with a little funk. For the rum, I like Smith & Cross for its full-on funky complexity, but it might be a little hard to find. Appleton Estate 12 is a good substitute (though I find that Appleton's younger rums are a little light in character for a shrubby drink).

INGREDIENTS

1¾ ounces Jamaican rum

¾ ounce Plum, Peppercorn, and Bay Leaf Shrub (page 159)

½ ounce lime juice

Lime wheel, for garnish

PROCESS

1. Add all ingredients except for garnish to an ice-filled cocktail shaker. Shake well until chilled.

2. Strain into a chilled cocktail glass. Add garnish.

THE BROOKLYN MANHATTAN

I'm sure you're familiar with the Manhattan cocktail, a blend of rye (or bourbon), sweet vermouth, and Angostura bitters, garnished with a cherry. The Manhattan gave rise to the Brooklyn, a variation that uses rye, dry vermouth, maraschino liqueur, and a bitter liqueur called Amer Picon. Generally speaking, this is how cocktail variations come about: take the sweet vermouth out and swap in dry; take the bitters out and add a bitter liqueur.

Starting about ten years ago, several New York City bartenders started creating variations on the Brooklyn. They'd take out the maraschino, say, and add Chartreuse. Or they'd take out the Amer Picon and use another bitter liqueur—Cynar, perhaps, or Campari. To name these drinks, they chose the names of Brooklyn neighborhoods: Bensonhurst, Bushwick, Carroll Gardens, Cobble Hill, Greenpoint, and Red Hook.

Ditmas Park

When you're a bartender (or for that matter, a cocktail writer) and you want to create a new drink, you can go about it in a couple of different ways. First, you can get totally creative and come up with something brand new, blending a little of this and a little of that until you find something flavorful and refreshing.

Or—and this is perhaps more common—you can adapt a classic. The Ditmas Park takes that approach. It's my adaptation on the Brooklyn cocktail, named for the neighborhood where my family lives.

INGREDIENTS

2 ounces rye

1 ounce dry vermouth

¼ ounce Fig-Cinnamon Shrub (page 106)

¼ ounce Averna Amaro

PROCESS

1. Add all ingredients to an ice-filled mixing glass, and stir until chilled.

2. Holding a tea strainer above a chilled cocktail glass, strain the drink through the tea strainer, so that any remaining fig seeds from the shrub are captured in the tea strainer.

El Canguro Picante

Many years ago, when I first visited New Orleans, I wasn't yet into cocktails. Though today I love drinking Sazeracs while in the Big Easy, I didn't have any idea what such a thing was at the time. Instead, I ordered a pepper martini, which wasn't much more than a chilled glass of Absolut Peppar, garnished with a slice of jalapeño.

I happen to occasionally enjoy an icy-cold vodka "martini," though I hold that the proper name for a vodka martini is a Kangaroo. I decided to re-create the pepper martini, using my Five-Pepper Shrub to provide the heat. This recipe makes enough for two, so find a friend. Also, you want everything as cold as possible, so carve out some space in your freezer.

INGREDIENTS

4 ounces vodka

1 ounce dry vermouth

¼ ounce Five-Pepper Shrub (page 140)

1¾ ounces water

Pickled jalapeño slices, for garnish

PROCESS

1. Combine vodka, vermouth, shrub, and water in a clean glass jar. Stash in the freezer for at least 6 hours. If you have room, place a couple of serving glasses in the freezer along with it.

2. Divide into 2 serving glasses. Add garnish.

Fennel Gibson

No one's really sure how the oniony alternative to the martini first arose, but my favorite story entails a teetotaler (some accounts say he was an American diplomat in Europe; others, a businessman) who ordered water in a cocktail glass to trick his drinking companions into thinking he was imbibing. To make the drink stand out as his on a serving tray full of martinis, this fellow requested his be garnished with an onion rather than an olive.

My version here calls for neither olive nor onion, but instead pickled fennel to complement the Fennel Shrub.

INGREDIENTS

2½ ounces gin

½ ounce dry vermouth

¼ ounce Fennel Shrub (page 154)

Pickled fennel, for garnish

PROCESS

1. Add ingredients to a mixing glass halfway full of ice.

2. Stir for 30 seconds.

3. Strain into chilled glass, and add garnish.

Gimlet

The origins of the gimlet are hard to pin down. One story says that it started aboard British naval vessels, as a way to fight scurvy. Ships would stock lime juice aboard for the antiscorbutic properties of the vitamin C. (If you read the history section of this book, this concept will sound familiar to you.) But lime juice isn't pleasant to drink on its own, and so naval officers would sweeten it with a little sugar and spike it with gin to make it palatable.

Who knows, really, what happened, and how the gimlet was born. What we know now is that the modern gimlet is normally made from gin and Rose's Lime Juice Cordial. Unfortunately, Rose's cordial is far too sweet for many drinkers. I propose we fix this problem by using something that has little backbone to it, namely lemon-lime shrub.

Feel free to tinker with this to your satisfaction; you might find that equal parts gin and shrub are not to your liking. It's your drink and your palate, so mix it the way you like.

INGREDIENTS

1½ ounces gin or vodka

1½ ounces Lemon-Lime Shrub (page 114)

PROCESS

1. Add ingredients to an ice-filled cocktail shaker. Shake until well chilled.

2. Strain into a chilled cocktail glass.

Gin Daisy

A Daisy is an old-school category of cocktail that's essentially a sour topped off with soda water. A Daisy calls for a base spirit, citrus juice, grenadine, and simple syrup. For those of you unfamiliar with grenadine—or for those who simply buy it from the mixers and soda aisle at your grocery and don't know what's in it—it's simply pomegranate syrup, flavored with a bit of orange flower water. For this version, we'll use pomegranate shrub in place of the grenadine and simple syrup.

INGREDIENTS

1½ ounces gin

½ ounce lemon juice

½ ounce Pomegranate Shrub (page 127)

Soda water

Lemon slice, for garnish

PROCESS

1. Add gin, lemon juice, and shrub to an ice-filled cocktail shaker.

2. Shake until chilled.

3. Strain over ice into a collins glass.

4. Top with soda water.

5. Add garnish.

NOTE

As is the case with a great many cocktails, the composition of the Daisy has changed over time. The original Daisy called for orange curaçao in place of the grenadine, and so you had a drink of a base spirit, citrus, and orange liqueur, topped with soda water. You can use any base in a Daisy—bourbon, rye, rum, vodka, blended scotch, or tequila—and the drink's name takes the spirit as its opener. So for example, a Daisy with bourbon is a Bourbon Daisy.

Or take a Tequila Daisy: Tequila, lime juice, and triple sec, topped with soda. Leave off the soda, and the drink might seem familiar to you. What's the Spanish for daisy? Why, it's *margarita*, of course.

LIBER & CO.

If you don't want to make Grapefruit Shrub for this recipe, try the one made by Liber & Co., an Austin, Texas, company that makes shrubs for bars and retail. The founders are Adam Higginbotham, Robert Higginbotham, and Chris Harrison, three longtime friends who turned their collective passion for cocktails into a small-batch cocktail ingredient company. They make concentrated syrups and shrubs that stay true to the craft and heritage of cocktails.

Liber experimented with flavors and techniques for several months prior to launching. They toyed with basic flavored sugar syrups but found them lacking intensity. By their nature, shrubs pack a larger punch due to their added acidity from vinegar. The first product was a rhubarb ginger shrub, made with champagne vinegar and cane sugar, which they debuted in Summer 2012. Liber's second product is a Texas-grapefruit shrub, made from Rio Star grapefruits unique to south Texas, plus coconut vinegar, cane sugar, and a touch of allspice.

Liber & Co. are expanding distribution in 2014. Your best bet right now is to order online at the Liber website (see Resources).

Greyhound

The classic Greyhound highball calls for vodka or gin and a tall pour of grape-fruit juice, somewhat like a screwdriver. You're certainly welcome to pour a shot of vodka into a glass and top it with shrub, but I think you might find that a little overwrought. Instead, I call for the vodka, and then a bit of shrub and some soda water. Much more balanced, I think.

INGREDIENTS

1½ ounces vodka or gin

1½ ounces Grapefruit Shrub (page 111)

Soda water

PROCESS

Add vodka (or gin) and shrub to an ice-filled collins glass. Top with soda water and stir.

Kir

My first, and thus far only, trip to Paris came in late 2001. I remember stopping
at a bistro for lunch, and I saw a Kir Royale on the menu. I was intrigued, so
I ordered it. Quite a tasty drink. The classic Kir is crème de cassis and white
wine. The Royale uses champagne in place of the wine. You can make a Kir
variation using just about any of the fruity shrubs in this book. Since cassis is
a black currant liqueur, using a currant shrub is a logical place to start, but you
don't need to limit yourself to that.

INGREDIENTS

½ ounce shrub of your
choice

3–4 ounces white wine or
champagne

PROCESS

Add shrub to a wine glass. Top with wine or champagne.

Moscow Mule

The Moscow Mule has a funny history. It was invented entirely for the purpose of selling two products: Smirnoff vodka and Cock 'N' Bull ginger beer. The now-defunct Heublein Brothers company first imported Smirnoff into the United States. One day in 1941, Heublein's president happened to be dining with the leader of Cock'n Bull Products. You see, strange as it may seem now, vodka wasn't always the spirits behemoth it is today, and Heublein was having trouble marketing it in the United States. So Smirnoff teamed up with Cock'n Bull to help both products reach a broader audience, and the Moscow Mule became a smash.

INGREDIENTS

2 ounces vodka

1 ounce fresh lime juice

¾ ounce Fresh Ginger Shrub (page 157)

Soda water

Lime wedges, for garnish

PROCESS

1. Pour vodka, lime juice, and shrub into an ice-filled copper mug.
2. Add soda water and stir.
3. Add garnish.

NOTE

The traditional vessel for a Moscow Mule is a copper mug. If you don't have such mugs, you can use a highball or collins glass. If you're interested in purchasing copper mugs, they're available at The Boston Shaker or Cocktail Kingdom. See Resources for more information.

Mrs. Wheelbarrow's Winter Martinez

This is adapted from a recipe by a friend of mine, Cathy Barrow. Cathy is a recipe developer and cooking instructor in the Washington, D.C., area. The martinez is a precursor to the martini, and it's usually made with gin and sweet vermouth. Cathy's original called for a fig balsamic vinegar instead of the shrub, but I like the shrub's complexity in this, and I really like the way it works with the gin and the vermouth. For the vermouth, I suggest something like Carpano Antica or Punt e Mes.

INGREDIENTS

2 ounces London dry gin

1 ounce sweet vermouth

½ ounce Fig-Cinnamon Shrub (page 106)

Orange peel, for garnish

PROCESS

1. Add all ingredients except garnish to an ice-filled mixing glass. Stir until well chilled.

2. Pour into a chilled cocktail glass.

3. Twist the orange peel over an open flame (a lighter is the best choice) to singe the oils. Drop the peel into the glass.

Peach Shandy

~~~~~~

Try this refreshing drink on a hot day. A shandy is a traditional quaff common under various names in Europe; it's simply a mix of beer with some sort of fruity nonalcoholic beverage, like lemonade, orange juice, or ginger ale.

~~~~~~

INGREDIENTS

2 ounces rye

1 ounce dry vermouth

¼ ounce Fig-Cinnamon Shrub (page 106)

¼ ounce Averna Amaro

PROCESS

1. Add all ingredients to an ice-filled mixing glass, and stir until chilled.

2. Holding a tea strainer above a chilled cocktail glass, strain the drink through the tea strainer, so that any remaining fig seeds from the shrub are captured in the tea strainer.

Pompier

Also known as the Vermouth Cassis, the Pompier is a French sidewalk-café classic, quite refreshing on hot summer days. The name, in fact, tells you what the drink is all about. Pompier is French for "firefighter." Even the original is low in alcohol, so a sophisticated Parisian could have repeated servings without melting onto the sidewalk. The original Pompier is a simple drink of crème de cassis (a currant liqueur) and French, or dry, vermouth (I like Dolin Blanc), topped with soda water. My version uses black currant shrub in place of the cassis, but frankly, any sweet berry shrub would work well in this.

INGREDIENTS

3 ounces dry vermouth

½ ounce Black Currant Shrub (page 91)

Soda water

PROCESS

1. Pour vermouth and shrub into an ice-filled collins glass.

2. Top with soda to taste.

Safe Harbor

You might have heard of a cocktail that calls for rum and ginger beer, and you might call it by the name Dark 'n Stormy. I remember the first time I had one, at a Caribbean restaurant in Manhattan, while dining with a group of friends. I passed my drink around the table for others to try, and nearly everyone ordered one of their own. The Dark 'n Stormy has an interesting history, though. The name of the drink is actually trademarked by the makers of Gosling's Black Seal Rum, from Bermuda, and the makers of Gosling's have been known to issue cease and desist orders to people who use the name to describe a drink that uses any rum other than Gosling's. It's not up to me to decide which rum you should use for this drink, so I've just taken it upon myself to rename the cocktail.

Besides, the Dark 'n Stormy is a classic highball: Gosling's and ginger beer. I'm fancying this up a tiny bit with some added lime juice. Gosling's would work well in this drink, but so would most other dark rums from the Caribbean.

INGREDIENTS

1½ ounces dark Caribbean rum

1½ ounces Fresh Ginger Shrub (page 157)

¾ ounce lime juice

Soda water

Lime wheel, for garnish

PROCESS

1. Pour rum, shrub, and lime juice into an ice-filled collins glass.

2. Add soda water and stir.

3. Add garnish.

Sangrita

The sangrita isn't really a cocktail, per se. Instead, it's a traditional way to drink tequila, arising from the Mexican state of Jalisco. Now, the original and perhaps the truest way to make sangrita is to take the juice of the Seville orange, blend that with lime and pomegranate juices, and then add chili powder or hot sauce. The chili powder gives the concoction a red color that reminded drinkers of blood, and in fact sangrita means "little blood."

The red color caused a misconception, that sangrita was made from tomato juice and lime, instead of orange and lime. Though purists might scoff at the tomato juice variant, I think it's delicious.

For the tequila, don't skimp. Find a good tequila, one that's 100 percent agave. You'll be sipping this, so you want it to taste good. Sangrita is not a shooter, and you're not in college anymore.

INGREDIENTS

1½ ounces blanco or reposado tequila

1½ ounces Tomato, Cilantro, and Coriander Shrub (page 176)

Dash chili powder, Tabasco, freshly minced chili peppers, or any spicy seasoning

PROCESS

1. Take two shot glasses. Fill one with tequila and the other with shrub. Add spice to shrub, to taste.

2. Sipping from each, alternate between the two. Take your time; the shrub will serve as a palate cleanser between sips of tequila.

Shrubby Mary

I have a few shrubs in this book that would taste great in a Bloody Mary. The Summer Tomato and Celery Shrub (page 171) already has the celery you're looking for in a Bloody, so that one's an obvious winner. Tomato, Cilantro, and Coriander Shrub (page 176) would add a South Asian approach to a Bloody. For a lighter, brighter version, try the Sungold Tomato and Basil Shrub (page 173). Finally, a Tomatillo Shrub Bloody Mary would be lovely, with all the clean citrus notes you associate with peak-season tomatillos (page 175).

INGREDIENTS

2 ounces vodka, gin, or aquavit (I prefer gin)

4 ounces Brandywine Tomato and Celery Shrub

¼ ounce lemon juice

¼ ounce lime juice

2 teaspoons prepared horseradish

2 dashes Angostura bitters

2 dashes Worcestershire sauce

1 dash Tabasco sauce

1 pinch ground black pepper

Lime wedge and stalk of celery, for garnish

PROCESS

1. Combine all ingredients (except garnish) in an ice-filled mixing glass. Take another glass, or the tin of a cocktail shaker, and gently pour the entire contents, ice and all, back and forth between the two vessels until the drink is well chilled.

2. Strain it into an ice-filled collins glass.

3. Add garnish.

NOTE

Why pour the drink from vessel to vessel instead of shaking it? Well, when you shake tomato shrub, it froths up and gets foamy. (This happens with tomato juice, too, and so I advise this technique for a standard Bloody Mary as well.) You could just stir everything together with ice in the serving glass, but you might find your ice melting too fast, making the drink weak and watery.

Shrubbed-Up Cosmo

Here we have a variant on the cosmopolitan, a drink that traditionally calls for citrus vodka, cranberry juice, lime juice, and Cointreau. I always feel that as a cocktail snob, I'm supposed to look down on the cosmo because Carrie Bradshaw made it famous, and if it's famous, it can't be good. Well, I actually somewhat enjoy the cosmo. Now, granted, I'd rather drink other things, but if a cosmo's in front of me, I'll enjoy it and won't gripe about it or feel guilty. Drinking is about having fun, not following a bunch of rules about what's cool and what's not. Here, I've taken the cosmo and shrubbed it up with a little apple-cranberry shrub. Enjoy!

INGREDIENTS

1½ ounces citrus vodka

¾ ounce Cointreau

½ ounce Cranberry-Apple Shrub (page 103)

¼ ounce fresh lime juice

Lime wedge, for garnish

PROCESS

1. Add all the ingredients except garnish to an ice-filled shaker. Shake well.

2. Strain into a chilled cocktail glass. Add garnish.

Shrugroniz

A Negroni is one of those classic drinks that I personally think everyone should love. It's an equal-parts mix of gin, sweet vermouth, and Campari bitter liqueur. Campari is an acquired taste, to be sure, but it's delicious. It's an Italian liqueur made from herbs and fruits; it tastes bitter and herbal and sweet, and it also has a very subtle fruitiness to it. Adding fruit shrub to a Negroni adds a bit of tartness from the vinegar and a bit of fruitiness, all balanced by a hint of sugar. You might find that you need to adjust the proportions a little on this cocktail to make it work for your palate, and that's perfectly fine. Just start with these proportions and adjust to your taste.

Negronis can be served either up (that is, stirred over ice and then strained into a cocktail glass) or on the rocks. I prefer the latter, but I've provided instructions for both.

INGREDIENTS

1 ounce London dry gin

1 ounce sweet vermouth

1 ounce Campari bitter liqueur

½ ounce fruit shrub of your choice

PROCESS

To serve up:

1. Add all ingredients to an ice-filled mixing glass. Stir until well chilled.

2. Strain into a chilled cocktail glass.

To serve on the rocks:

1. Add several ice cubes into a rocks glass. Add all ingredients, and then stir until well chilled.

Ultramodern

~~~~~~

This variation on an old-fashioned stars bourbon and scotch, with fig-cinnamon shrub providing the sweetener, and Angostura bitters rounding out the drink. It's the perfect final recipe.

~~~~~~

INGREDIENTS

2 ounces bourbon

½ ounce scotch, preferably something smoky, like Laphroaig

½ ounce Fig-Cinnamon Shrub (page 106)

2 dashes Angostura bitters

PROCESS

1. Add all ingredients to an ice-filled mixing glass. Stir to combine.

2. Double-strain into a rocks glass filled with ice.

APPENDIX

SUGGESTED FLAVOR COMBINATIONS FOR MAKING YOUR OWN SHRUBS

APPLE

- Cinnamon
- Cranberry
- Ginger

APRICOTS

- Rosemary
- Cardamom
- Chamomile

BLOOD ORANGE

- Clove

BLUEBERRY

- Lavender

CARROT

- Anise

GRAPEFRUIT

- Basil
- Mint
- Rosemary
- Thyme

KIWI

- Coconut

MELON

- Lemongrass
- Lemon verbena

NECTARINE

- Cilantro

SAFETY

The following tips are adapted from "Preserving Food: Flavored Vinegars," a pamphlet from the National Center for Home Food Preservation (NCHFP) and the University of Georgia Cooperative Extension Service:

1. *Prepare your jars or bottles.* The NCHFP suggests using only glass containers for storing vinegars. Wash them well, and then add them carefully to a deep pot. Completely cover them with water, turn on the stove, and bring the water to a boil. Boil for 10 minutes. Remove the jars from the water, drain the water out of them, and fill while they're still warm.

2. *Prepare your fruit.* Prepare a sanitizing solution of vinegar and water. Add 1 tablespoon distilled white vinegar to 6 cups of water. Soak the fruit in the solution for 10 minutes, rinse, and drain until mostly dry.

3. *Prepare your herbs,* if you're following a recipe that calls for them, such as Blueberry Lavender Shrub. Fresh herbs can attract all sorts of microbes, so if you want to be as safe as possible, you might want to disinfect them. First, wash them well and gently, so as not to damage the herbs. Make a sanitizing solution of 1 teaspoon chlorine beach to 6 cups of water. Dip the herbs in the sanitizing solution, rinse under cold water, and blot dry with paper towels.

RESOURCES

SHRUB MAKERS

Shrub makers seem to be popping up about one a month these days. I was able to profile three for this book, but here I'm including information for a few more. Also, keep your eye peeled at your local farmers' market or specialty food store. You might have a shrub maker in your community that I don't even know about yet.

BITTERMENS
www.bittermens.com

BUG HILL FARM
www.bughillfarm.org

LIBER & CO.
www.liberandcompany.com

MAD MAIDEN SHRUB
www.madmaidenshrub.com

SHRUB & CO.
www.shrubandco.com

TAIT FARM FOODS
www.taitfarmfoods.com

BARWARE, SHRUBS, AND COCKTAIL INGREDIENTS

THE BOSTON SHAKER

www.thebostonshaker.com

COCKTAIL KINGDOM

www.cocktailkingdom.com

KEGWORKS

www.kegworks.com

THE MEADOW

www.atthemeadow.com

VINEGARS

CHAPARRAL GARDENS

www.chaparralgardens.com

FIORE ARTISAN OLIVE OILS AND VINEGARS

www.fioreoliveoils.com

SPICE TRADERS MERCANTILE

www.spicetradersmercantile.com

TAVERN VINEGAR

www.tavernvinegar.com

ACKNOWLEDGMENTS

This book started in a surprising way. I was walking my son home from the playground one spring morning. I checked my email en route and saw a new message titled, "Want to write a book?" The sender was my now-editor, Ann Treistman, with an idea for a book about shrubs. Thank you, Ann, for taking a chance on a neophyte author and helping me figure out how the hell to write a book.

I want to thank everyone at Countryman Press who ushered along this book, especially Nick Caruso for his beautiful design; Bill Rusin and Michael Levatino for pushing this book in sales; and Laura Stiers for her thorough and precise copyediting. I've worked as a copyeditor; I worked hard to make the road straight and smooth for Laura, but nobody's perfect, and she filled every pothole and tightened every wayward curve.

After Ann's first email message, I then contacted my editor at Serious Eats, Maggie Hoffman, even before I said anything to my wife. I wanted to let Maggie know early on that my weekly deadline might suffer. (Luckily, it didn't. At least, not very often.) I owe Maggie my gratitude for being patient and excited about this project. To my surprise, Maggie also suggested an agent, the talented and tenacious Vicky Bijur. As a first-time author, I would have been at sea without Vicky.

I can't remember when I first heard of shrubs, but I do remember an illuminating conversation, during a seminar at Tales of the Cocktail, between the writer Paul Clarke and the bartender Neyah White about pairing shrubs with aperitif wines to produce low-alcohol cocktails. Thanks, Paul and Neyah, for a great seminar, and thanks again, Paul, for your words of advice while I was writing the book.

I want to thank Claudia Young, of Cleveland's Velvet Tango Room, for explaining how the VTR uses shrubs in its cocktails, and for providing a couple of recipes. Thanks, too, to Cathy Barrow, Charlie Crebs, and Niklas Morris for contributing recipes.

I want to thank everyone from Tait Farm Foods, Liber & Co., and Shrub & Co. for your time and attention, especially near the end when we were bugging you for photos.

Fred Yarm explained the chemistry of shrub making, and I hope he'll be pleased to see his words writ large on these pages.

For their unending support and encouragement, I want to thank the aforementioned Cathy Barrow, plus Meriko Borogove, Anita Crotty, Gail Dosik, Amanda Hathaway, Robert Haynes-Peterson, Robert and Nancy Hess, Lindsey Johnson, Alexander Kern, Adam Lantheaume, Hanna Lee, and Kara Newman. Also, my mother, Patricia Dietsch.

Finally, my wife, Jennifer Hess, took most of the lovely photographs you've seen in these pages. For many of our photo shoots, she was pregnant with our second child, climbing onto step stools and kneeling on the floor to get the perfect shot. The work was physically and mentally demanding, the author didn't always know what the hell he wanted, and the eldest child sometimes intruded into the viewfinder. The English language does not contain enough words to express my gratitude.

INDEX

Note: *Italicized* page references indicate recipe photographs.
Boldfaced page references indicate where shrub is used as an ingredient.